Key's ABC'S to Leadership

*26 Principles for a Better Life
Personally and Professionally*

Mansfield Key III

Copyright © 2015 by Mansfield Key III.

All Rights Reserved.

Without prior permission in writing from the publisher, no portion of this publication may be reproduced, stored in retrieval system, or transmitted in any form by any means, electronic or mechanical, including photocopying, recording, or by any other information storage and retrieval system, except for brief quotations in printed reviews.

Library of Congress

This book was derived from a workshop for leaders that was originally entitled: "Putting the Pieces Together"

Cover layout and book designed by Dede Simmons, Ultimate Graphix

ISBN # 978-1-4951-3961-1

DEDICATION

Every good work requires the effort of a group of individuals. This project is no exception to the rule.

This book is dedicated to all the great writers in my family – my mother, Shirley Key, my grandmother, Geneive Dortch Brown, and my Great Grandfather, Stroke "Pappa" Dortch. They all passed away before they got to write their books. I thank them for their gifts and I hope that I am able to pass on the wisdom that they gave to me.

To my wife, Sharlene, who has been my friend, my love, and my biggest supporter since middle school. To my daughters, Erin and Joi, for their understanding and patience when I was up working until 3:00 AM. To my brothers, Roderick and Derric "Tank" Key, for believing that their brother could write more than rap songs. Special thanks to my Dad, Mansfield Key, Jr., the most avid reader I know. Thank you, Pop, for helping to mold me into the man I am today.

I dedicate this to the team of people who allowed me to lead them while I was still learning the leadership principles that I share in this book. Special thanks to Anthony "AB" Brooks for putting the finishing touches on what I thought was complete. To the dream team of Latasha Howell, Lois Jackson, Dede Simmons, Dr. D. Peterson, Sarah Deuoron

Perry, James Edwards, and Tangela Butler – words can't express my gratitude. Thank you to Jeremy Anderson for giving me guidance in the world of publishing. Thanks to my mentors, Dr. Rozario Slack, TJ Johnson, and Bishop David Richey. Many thanks to the behind the scenes team of Sepia Gladden, Bishop Eddie Long, Pastors Brady and Vickie Butler, Pastor Margaret Richey, Anthony Toney Jordan, Terrell Brown, Mrs. Stockard, Billy Ray Casteel, Dr. Jimmy Shaw, Eugene Sak, Roderick Shepphard, Joyce Greene, Pastor Aota Acts and my Grace Chapel Family of Johannesburg, South Africa, Michelle Dawes-Birt, Angela Sheppard-Smalls, Patricia "Bridget" Watts, and Barbara Jackson, Terrell Butler and many others. And last, but not least, Kyle Buckley, the "Dream Writer" for editing this book.

As an author whose teacher used to refer to him as the "kid that couldn't read," I dedicate this to the students, and to anyone who ever believed that they couldn't succeed because someone once told them that they didn't "have what it takes."

I dedicate this to all the things that you will do to defy the odds.

CONTENTS

Introduction 1
Prologue 5
How to Read the 26 Keys 13
Chapter 1 - Attitude, Affirmation, Accountability 17
Chapter 2 - Believing, Building, Balancing 27
Chapter 3 - Communicate, Collaborate, Commit 35
Chapter 4 - Dedicated, Disciplined, Determined 43
Chapter 5 - Exposed, Educated, Empowered 49
Chapter 6 - Faithful, Focused, Fruitful 55
Chapter 7 - Guts, Growth, Gifts 61
Chapter 8 - Humble, Hopeful, Heart-Centered 69
Chapter 9 - Invest, Impact, Inspire 77
Chapter 10 - Journaling, Joinable, Joyful 83
Chapter 11 - Knowledge, Kindness, Know-How 89
Chapter 12 - Looking, Listening, Learning 95
Chapter 13 - Methods, Motives, Mission 103
Chapter 14 - Network, Navigate, Negotiate 111
Chapter 15 - Options, Outlets, Opportunities 117
Chapter 16 - Persistence, Planning, Positivity 125
Chapter 17 - Quality, Qualifications, Quintessence 133
Chapter 18 - Relatable, Reliable, Real 141
Chapter 19 - Service, Strength, Success 147
Chapter 20 - Teachable, Truthful, Team-Oriented 153
Chapter 21 - Understanding, Unique, Uplifting 161
Chapter 22 - Visualize, Verbalize, Validate 167
Chapter 23 - Wisdom, Willingness, Work Ethic 175
Chapter 24 - X-ray 183
Chapter 25 - Yearn, Yes, Yield 189
Chapter 26 - Zesty, Zealous, Zany 195
Epilogue 201

INTRODUCTION

"If we could change ourselves, the tendencies in the world would also change. As a man changes his own nature, so does the attitude of the world change towards him... We need not wait to see what others do."
- Mahatma Gandhi

What is a leader? The dictionary describes a leader as a person who leads or commands a group, organization, or country; a guiding or directing head, as of an army, movement, or political group. The late, great Dr. Myles Monroe describes leadership as, "a person's capacity to influence others through inspiration, motivated by a passion, generated by a vision, produced by a conviction, ignited by a purpose." Some leaders say that leadership is pure influence. Others say that the ultimate leader is a servant.

There are leaders who serve and leaders who want to be served. There are leaders who have a title and a position, but have no real influence outside of the title. Then there are leaders who don't have the title or position, but possess a power to lead through their capacity to truly impact and influence others. Some have a natural gift and talent for leadership, and their ability positions them to lead. Some are placed into a leadership position and then given the opportunities to develop leadership skills. And still others are driven to lead by necessity, accepting responsibility and stepping up to the plate when no one else will.

Weak leaders with a strong vision can do more than strong leaders with no vision. If a leader has no vision, then he has nowhere to lead people, no matter how strong his influence or charisma may be. Even if someone doesn't possess all the skills and qualities of an effective leader, their commitment to a vision allows them to attract what they don't yet have.

I say that the most essential defining characteristic of a leader is a strong commitment to personal and professional growth. Through a commitment to growth, all of the key skills and characteristics of a leader can be cultivated and acquired.

Are you a leader? How do you know that you're a leader? Who told you that you are a leader? Did getting a position and a title make you a leader, or was it a deeper cultivation of the skills that it takes to lead? Did becoming a parent give you the skills and knowledge to wisely guide your child? Did becoming a teacher equip you with the skills to lead a classroom? Before you can ever lead anyone, remember that the hardest person to lead is yourself. The question is who and what are you allowing to influence and lead you?

Key's ABC's of Leadership

PROLOGUE

My Personal Path to Leadership

My name is Mansfield Key III, and I am a leader. I never asked to be a leader. I didn't win an election or give a speech to my peers and ask their permission to be their leader. I never completed an application or took a training course for the job of leader. So how did I become a leader? I became a leader when someone told me that I was one and I chose to step up to the plate.

It was during the Christmas holidays, I was in seventh grade, five of us guys on the basketball team decided to skip practice. As a consequence, our coach told us that we would each have to sit out a game, and he would decide which one. One of the guys, the group ringleader, convinced all of us that we should quit the team instead of accepting coach's punishment. The idea was if we refused the punishment and quit the team, then coach would only have five players left. Since that wasn't a full team, we thought he would be forced to let us stay.

By the time we got back to school, the word was out that five guys might quit the team. One person on the team was about to decide the fate for the rest of us. It was the last class period of the day and we were getting ready for practice. Coach asked, "Do you guys understand why you have to sit out a game?" We all said, "Yes, Coach, we understand." Coach asked if any of us had anything to say. I said, "Yes, Coach. I want to tell you I'm sorry I disobeyed the rules and I'm willing to accept any punishment. Thank you for letting me stay on the team." Everyone looked at me funny, and then my best friend said, "Coach, I want to say I'm sorry I didn't show up to practice." Eventually, everyone apologized and stayed on the team, including the ringleader.

After that incident, my classmates and teammates started looking to me as a leader. Initially, we all went along with the ringleader's plan because he was a bully. We were scared of him. To the rest of the guys, it looked as if I had stood up to him, but that wasn't the whole truth. The truth was that my dad told me that I had to apologize as soon as I saw the coach and accept whatever punishment came my way, or I could look forward to a good whipping when I got home. My actions appeared bold to the guys. In reality, when it came down to facing my dad with all of his authority and power, versus a 120 pound seventh grader, there really wasn't a question as to whose directive I would follow.

I learned a key lesson about leadership that day. I had believed that leadership was based on position, but I found out that it was based on influence. I may have been trying to save my 13-year-old skin, but what I discovered was that, despite my selfish motives, I had a capacity to positively influence others. As a result, I can honestly say that from that day to this one I have been operating as a leader. However, not always in a postive way.

I was the lead fork lift operator when I worked at a production plant, and I led the truck drivers and the other fork lift operators. When I was in college, I held another job as an order puller at a golf supply company. That same golf company promoted me to assistant shipping and receiving supervisor, and they later put me in charge of motivating and managing coworkers for maximum productivity. I was the Director and Founder of the FAMILY Program in the Florence City School System. As a social service worker, I created a program to get non-custodial fathers involved in the educational process of their children. I've been trained and certified in Effective Climate for Leadership, 21st Century Community Learning Centers Program, and the National Fatherhood Initiative, to name a few.

Today, I'm an entrepreneur with a gift and a passion to help people. I have motivated people all over the world, from the United States, Africa and Europe. As a

Growth Development Strategist, my purpose and passion is to support people to become their best by developing strategies to lead a more fulfilling and productive life. Although I have held many leadership positions within a variety of industries, it didn't prepare me for the ultimate role as a leader.

Leader of a Family

Every leadership role I've held has required high performance, work ethic, positive attitude, and character. To fulfill my ultimate leadership role as a father and husband required all of that and much, much more. It has been my most rewarding and challenging leadership role thus far. It has brought out the worst and the best in me. Having a family has challenged and inspired the way that I do what I do as a leader and, most importantly, my reasons for doing it.

There isn't a trophy for being father or husband of the year. You get no accolades, you don't win any trip, and you don't get a raise or a bonus for high achievement. It's not always pretty. The Bible says that a good father leaves an inheritance for his children's children, which means that my job as a father is to be such a positive influence on the lives of my children that their children also receive the benefits.

Being a father has taught me more about leading by example than anything else that I've done. Leaders want to be validated, appreciated, and supported, but first they must be willing to validate, appreciate, and support others. As leaders, sometimes we are guilty of demanding or requesting things that we aren't willing to do ourselves, and my family makes sure that I never get away with that. Being a husband and father has taught me that, when it comes to being a positive influence for change in this world, it all comes back to quality of character and personal growth, and the small things matter much more than we can ever imagine.

Whether you're leading a company, a school, a classroom, a sports team, a ministry, or a family of three, this book will help you to lead by teaching you to lead yourself.

Leadership Training

Becoming a leader is a lifelong training. It's a commitment to a path that will challenge and empower you to grow more than you ever have before. To reach your goals and grow fully into your gifts, you will need support, mentorship, and guidance along the way. As a service and support to those who have committed themselves to this journey of a lifetime, I've created a full series of leadership training materials to support you in becoming the leader you were born to be. In addition to this book, I also offer:

· *Key's ABC's to Leadership* DVD Training – three full length DVDs that include an entire live training session that will enlighten leaders with the powerful tools they need to lead more effectively

· *Key's ABC's to Leadership* CD – a 28 track CD that brings an in-depth insight to each of the leadership Keys that you won't find on the DVD or in the book. Full of stories, quotes, and principles that will enhance your leadership in creative and empowering ways.

· *Key's ABC's to Leadership* 52 Week Challenge – Created to accompany the CD and the book, the 52 Week Challenge asks leaders to commit to a different activity each week for a total of 52 weeks. By the end of the challenge, you will not only understand the *Keys to Leadership* – you will be living them.

This book, DVD training, audio expansion, and action step guide will give you a clear picture of the steps you need to follow to arrive at the greatest view of you. You can find out more about these materials and further trainings at www.keysabcs.com.

Thank you for choosing to step up, stand out, and lead the way. The world is waiting for you.

Key's ABC's of Leadership

HOW TO READ THE 26 KEYS

This book was born through my own journey into leadership. What started as a PowerPoint presentation for a leadership training that shared my personal views has grown into much, much more. Although this is not a personal memoir of the stories of my successes and failures as a professional and father, it does apply much of what I've learned through that journey as practical and profound leadership lessons. The principles that I share are the vital lessons and keys that any leader can use to be successful as a person and as a professional.

Certain leadership characteristics are specific to particular fields, but there are qualities and principles that apply across the board, such as good work ethic, passion, character, and a positive attitude. The pages that follow will cover all of this and more through the 26 Keys, which offer practical guidance, insight, and approaches that can be applied to any area of your life, and that will help to build you into the leader you are meant to be.

Each chapter is a journey in itself. With each letter of the alphabet, we'll go through a story with living examples that illustrate the core lessons of that letter. From there, I offer an outline of the principles for that letter along with the actions a leader must take to live those principles. Then, the chapter finishes with a list of three key things that I wish I would have known before I became a leader – lessons that I learned the hard way turned into priceless guidance for others. To finish out each chapter, I ask some guiding questions and leave space for you to write out your notes and reflections.

You can go through the book sequentially, or jump from chapter to chapter if there are certain principles that you want to work on right away. Whatever order you choose, to get the most out of this book I recommend going through each chapter fully and spending some time with the reflections before you move on to the next. Always ask yourself: how can I act on and apply what I've learned?

Your leadership journey is entirely unique to you, so it's up to you to take the practical knowledge and wisdom within these pages and transform yourself and your life. A leader is someone who holds others accountable and, most importantly, holds themselves accountable. My prayer is that this book moves you to lead the way for greater growth, good, and success in yourself and in everything that you do. Just remember this important K.E.Y.:

KNOWLEDGE EMPOWERS YOU.

Now it's up to you to use the power for the greater good. I wish you only the best.

Key's ABC's of Leadership

"A bad attitude is like a flat tire. If you don't change it, you will never go anywhere." - Unknown

ATTITUDE, AFFIRMATION, ACCOUNTABILITY

As a leader, you must be able to adapt your attitude and action strategy to your surroundings, sometimes at a moment's notice. There's a great example of this in the game of football. Most quarterbacks are the offensive leaders on their team. The quarterback is sometimes known as "the coach on the field," and he's the one responsible for executing the play on the field. He gets the play from the coach, who is on the sideline, and then gives it to the other players in the huddle. Once the players break from the huddle, they get ready to execute the play and go to the line of scrimmage. The quarterback goes underneath the center to run the play, and at this point, he may notice something. If the quarterback senses that the play they have called won't work because of the way the defense is positioned, then he has an option. Instead of running the play that the coach called, he can change the play at the line of scrimmage. He has to act quickly, because he has a 30 second window to run the play or get called for a delay of game. In that moment that he sees an opening for a better play, the quarterback can call out a code to his teammates signaling the new play and shift the team into a more advantageous position. This is known as "calling an audible."

> **Leaders must be willing to alter, adjust, and adapt their attitude to the atmosphere they encounter.**

Leaders can call an audible in any professional or personal situation. It's important that leaders have the capacity to see and sense their environment. A leader must be aware and alert as to what is taking place, and then have the ability and authority to shift their plan of action accordingly. If an atmosphere of disbelief, doubt, and discouragement is present, leaders can shift that atmosphere simply by adjusting and adapting their attitude.

Attitudes are contagious. When you call an audible on your attitude, it means that you are changing the atmosphere with your thoughts, words, or actions. Why is this a vital leadership skill? Life is unpredictable. We have to be ready for the times when we walk into the office, the church, the school, our house and find that the atmosphere is not suited for whatever plan we had laid out. What if a supervisor walked into the office ready to give instructions and found the manager crying because her husband had just been diagnosed with cancer? Or what if a teacher walked into the classroom to give a test and found his students in an uproar because someone had just gotten into a fight in the hallway?

In those moments, a great leader knows how to call an audible and address the issues at hand. That means being able to shift the game plan at a moment's notice by being able to change the plan of action, stopping and reversing a negative momentum while maintaining a positive attitude.

A leader can always offer positive affirmation over negative expectations. Leaders must be able to tell the difference between an ANT (Automatic Negative Thinker) and an APP (Affirming Positive Person). We have all had days when negative thoughts take over. We've all had days when it's been easier to look at all the things that are going wrong instead of being grateful for everything that's going right. We always have a choice between focusing on what we don't have and what we can't do, or focusing on what we do have and what we can do. Being an ANT will keep you in that place unless you get some APPs.

An APP will help you to see the positive in everything. An APP will remind you that you're strong when you feel weak and will make you feel like you can do anything, even when it seems impossible. As APPs, leaders feed the internal mental spirit of a person and take the focus off the external. Surrounding yourself with APPs ensures the success of any endeavor, and being an Affirming Positive Person starts with just one person, and that's you. You must choose to build positive momentum for yourself.

> ANT (Automatic Negative Thinker) and an APP (Affirming Positive Person).

Leaders must be able to affirm the people who they are leading in positive and productive ways. Everyone wants to feel that their actions and contributions are appreciated. When people feel affirmed in what they are doing, it increases their willingness to let their leader hold them accountable.

Accountability is a term that some leaders love and some leaders hate. Unfortunately, some leaders love to apply that word to the people who they're leading, but hate to use it on themselves. Every position of authority is accountable to a greater authority. For instance, students are held accountable by their teachers, the teachers by the principals, the principals by the district, and the district by the state board, and so on. To effectively hold others accountable, you must be willing to be accountable to others, and most important of all, to yourself.

The A's of Leadership

Leaders must be willing to alter, adjust, and adapt their attitude to the atmosphere they encounter.

Leader's attitudes are contagious. Therefore, the aroma of their attitude should be a sweet fragrance of positive affirmation on negative expectation.

When leaders enter an atmosphere of disbelief, doubt, and discouragement, they can disarm the situation and shift it with their attitude.

Leaders who have problems holding people accountable are usually having problems being accountable.

Effective leaders acknowledge and affirm their strengths and the strengths of their team. They also acknowledge their own weaknesses, as well as the weaknesses of their team.

When leaders acknowledge what they cannot do, they create the opportunity to delegate and designate someone who may be better at the task. This allows the team to grow stronger.

Leaders must be able to achieve and accomplish goals that they set for themselves and their team.

Leaders are responsible to their team to create a plan of action, but they may not be in control of the outcome.

Leaders who have achieved and accomplished success in any area are people who did not quit when they faced adversity.

Leaders are alert, aware, and available to the people they lead.

Leaders know that a small pint of encouragement and affirmation can lead to gallons of accomplishments, accolades, and achievements.

Leaders recognize that there is no perfect time for change because action has no season.

Leaders know that even when they are afraid, they cannot abandon or abort the activity.

Three things that I wish I would have known about leadership before I became a leader:

1. Be willing to alter, adjust, and adapt.

2. Be alert, aware, and available.

3. Be accessible and action-oriented.

Guiding Questions

Is your attitude welcomed into the atmosphere, or do people dread seeing you come into the room?

Do you know how to shift and call an audible on your

attitude to change the atmosphere?

Are you rejecting being held accountable while trying to hold others accountable?

Chapter 1 – Key Insights & Reflections

CHAPTER 2

"There's no such thing as work-life balance. There are work-life choices, and you make them, and they have consequences." - Jack Welch

BELIEVING, BUILDING, BALANCING

Sometimes, leaders are so busy building that they forget to balance being busy with being truly blessed. Having good health, good relationships, and a joyful heart are all blessings. I've known many leaders who focus so much of their energy on building their professional lives that they lose the people closest to them. This struggle can be even harder for women in the workforce who take on the task of balancing work with being the primary caregivers in their family.

Balancing is not always easy, and it requires a unique skillset. A classic leadership question is: which comes first, the project or the people? The answer is that different situations require different priorities. Leaders must know how to balance being relational and people-oriented with being firmly focused on the project at hand.

I remember when I was first starting out as a speaker trying to build my audience. I was so excited and eager to get on stage that when someone called, I didn't know how to say no. I found myself going almost 6 days a week, traveling, speaking, building my business, and changing the world. After a couple of months of this, I realized that I was putting more energy into work than I was into my family. In that moment, I knew that I had to re-balance my priorities. To be productive, leaders must be able to balance their professional demands with their personal demands. Even if you have the skills, the heart and the ability to lead, if you live out of balance for too long, it will undermine your success.

> Effective leaders never pass the buck or the blame onto their team while they boast and brag about themselves.

When it comes to the people-oriented aspect of a leader's work, the most important skill a leader can cultivate is the capacity to believe in others. This became incredibly clear to me during a speech that I gave in a community center in Johannesburg, South Africa. I asked the people there a simple question: what have you always dreamed of doing or becoming? They looked at me like I'd just cursed in church. After a long moment of silence, one little girl asked me a question that has stuck with me for years. She asked, "How do you believe for better when everything around looks hopeless?" I told her and everyone in the room that the ability to see beyond where you are is the greatest gift anyone could ever possess. Helen Keller said, "The most pathetic person in the world is someone who has sight, but no vision." Even though she couldn't see physically, Helen Keller could see tremendous possibilities.

Great leaders can get people to "believe for better" when they begin to believe for themselves. Believing in people brings out the best in them. By doing just this one thing, a leader can inspire people to go places and do things that they would have never attempted on their own.

The B's of Leadership

Leaders know how to balance family, profession, fitness,

and finances.

Leaders must be able to build their dreams, and this comes with building their personal and professional brand.

Sometimes leaders get so busy building that they forget to balance being busy with being truly blessed.

Leaders are able to believe the impossible, know how to build it, and get others to believe it and build it with them.

Leaders don't have time to be lazy - they must be busy working when it's time to work so that they can play when it's time to play.

Leaders must be able to balance being task-oriented with being people-oriented. Leaders should always do their best and try to bring out the best in others.

Leaders have to believe in their followers to help their followers to believe in themselves.

Leaders must be able to believe that it's possible, even when what they are dreaming for seems impossibly far off.

Leaders know that people should be treated as if they are who they are destined to become, even while they're in the process of becoming.

Leaders are constantly becoming better at leading because they are always learning.

Effective leaders never pass the buck or the blame onto their team while they boast and brag about themselves.

Three things that I wish I would have known about leadership before I became a leader:

1. A leader helps people to see beyond where they are currently.

2. A leader shows people that they can do more than they are currently doing.

3. A leader empowers people to fuel the future instead of feeding the present.

Guiding Questions

Where can you bring more balance to your life? Where is your balance weak, and where is your balance strong?

How do you "believe for better," and how do you get the people who you lead to "believe for better"?

Chapter 2 – Key Insights & Reflections

Leaders must challenge the process because any system will unconsciously conspire to maintain the status quo." - Andy Stanley

COMMUNICATE, COLLABORATE, COMMIT

My first year as the director of the FAMILY Program taught me some huge lessons in leadership. This was a Fatherhood Program designed to get Head Start fathers involved in their child's education. I was so excited about the position and the prestige that came with the title that I overlooked the full responsibility required. I was committed to the cause, but I didn't understand how many people I would have to collaborate, communicate, and cooperate with to make it successful.

During that first school year, only two fathers volunteered for a total of nine hours. The entire year was a complete disaster. The second year was a little bit better, but it wasn't until the third year that I realized that my method of getting information to the fathers wasn't working, and that I needed to create a direct connection with them.

In order to get different results, I had to have the courage to change what I was doing. Once I learned how to communicate, collaborate, and cooperate with others, I witnessed great progress. We went from being the worst program in the state to receiving the state award for "Program of the Year." To create the desired outcome, leaders must be able to see what's not working and then change it.

All leaders should have the courage to either create their own vision or carry out the vision that is set before them. Then, they must be able to effectively communicate the vision to their team, along with setting a clear pathway for bringing that vision into reality. The first step is commitment to the cause.

> Leaders must be able to meet complaints, criticism, controversy, and conflict with confidence and commitment to the cause.

A leader will face obstacles and setbacks along the

way, but where there is commitment to a cause, there is strength to continue. As Zig Ziglar said, "It was character that got us out of bed, commitment that moved us into action and discipline that enabled us to follow through."

It is through collaborating with others that we can accomplish our goals. Leaders know that they must cooperate and collaborate, and they also need to be coachable and approachable. Collaborating, communicating, and cooperating with others will help to foster greater connection, which leads to greater partnerships. When leaders are connected to the people who they're leading, it allows for better communication and increased understanding, even when there are differing points of view.

The C's of Leadership

Leaders must be competent and capable of leading themselves before they can lead others.

Leaders must be coachable and approachable in order to effectively coach others.

Leaders understand that the courage to change starts with

confessing the need for change.

Leaders should have the courage to stay committed to the cause and continue on in the face of challenge and conflict.

To effectively lead in the era and the arena they have chosen, leaders must be willing to change with the times.

Leaders are conscious of the vision they're carrying and of what it will cost to create it and cultivate it.

Leaders are willing to resolve conflict and confront the issues that are keeping them from progressing.

Leaders know how to calculate the cost of the journey and determine whether it's worth it.

Leaders understand the necessity of collaborating with others to accomplish their goals.

Leaders choose to cooperate and work together, even when they may not see eye- to-eye.

Leaders who collaborate, communicate, and cooperate can use connection to resolve conflict more quickly.

Leaders must be able to clearly and concisely communicate their ideas and expectations so that everyone knows what they're being asked to do.

When leaders are connected to their people, they have a better rapport, which creates mutual understanding between them and the people who they're leading.

Leaders must have the courage to follow their personal convictions, even when others do not agree.

Leaders should not complain about what they've been commissioned to change.

Leaders create a culture and climate with a ceiling that allows them to compete with themselves instead of others.

Leaders have the courage to commit to their career and calling with confidence.

Leaders must be able to meet complaints, criticism, controversy, and conflict with confidence and commitment to the cause.

Three things that I wish I would have known about leadership before I became a leader:

1. Choose the necessary change with confidence.

2. Commit to the cause and pay the cost.

3. Collaborate, communicate, and cooperate with others.

Guiding Questions

Are you close enough to the people you're leading to sense what frustrates them the most?

Are you far enough ahead of the people you're leading so that you can increase their capacity for growth?

Chapter 3 – Key Insights & Reflections

"True dedication and discipline connects today's actions to tomorrow's results." - Unknown

DEDICATED, DISCIPLINED, DETERMINED

Day in and day out, leaders must be dedicated to the work at hand. In my work, I'm often reminded of the proverbial saying that sometimes, it's hard to see the forest for the trees. Good leaders have the capacity to see both the forest and the trees, and know when and where to focus their vision. When leading a group of people, sometimes it's more important to keep attention on the details and specifics of the task at hand. At other times, the team may need to be reminded of the big picture in order to stay inspired and focused during a difficult moment. Having direction, dedication, and discipline is the key to this process.

Leaders know how to dedicate themselves to self-discipline. If you want to grow, then you must be determined. That means being willing to put in the time, money, and energy that the growth process requires. If you want the degree, then you have to go back to school. If you want the power and prestige, you must apply the self-discipline that's needed to reach your goal.

A few years ago, I set a weight loss goal for myself. I was exercising daily and working with a personal trainer. After one month, I still hadn't lost any weight and was feeling really discouraged. I talked to my trainer, and he asked me the one question that I didn't want to answer: what are you eating? He reminded me that it didn't make sense to do the exercise if I couldn't be self-disciplined about my eating habits. At that moment, I realized that if I was determined to reach my goal of having a physically fit body, I'd have to step up my dedication to the discipline that it would take to get there.

> **Leaders must be able to define, design, develop, and demonstrate the plan of action.**

In any leadership journey, whether it's in your personal life or professional life, you will face obstacles and challenges. If you know this starting out, then you can choose to be determined to stay the course regardless of what comes up along the way.

The D's of Leadership

Leaders are dedicated to the work at hand each and every day.

Leaders have the discipline and determination to stay the course, even when the going gets difficult.

If leaders are not dedicated, disciplined and determined, they will get distracted and delayed and make a detour away from destiny, toward destruction.

Leaders know that some people succeed because they are destined. They also know destiny is made real through dedication, discipline and determination.

Leaders must be aware of the diversions of all shapes and sizes that come up to distract them from their daily course.

Leaders are dedicated to growth and development for themselves, and for the people they're leading.

Leaders must be able to define, design, develop, and demonstrate the plan of action.

Leaders are gifted with an ability to develop plans and also to develop people by giving them directions to get to where they want to go.

Leaders develop other leaders.

True leaders discipline themselves to lead by example.

Effective leaders complete and develop trust in others while ineffective leaders compete and destroy trust in others.

Three things that I wish I would have known about leadership before I became a leader:

1. Leaders are dedicated to developing themselves so they can develop others.

2. Distractions can lead to delays; delays can lead to detours; and detours can lead to destruction.

3. Dedication, determination, and discipline will keep leaders headed in the right direction when the going gets difficult.

Guiding Questions

Are you desiring something that you are not willing to discipline and dedicate yourself to achieving?

Have you developed a mental roadmap to success for your corporation, school, or life?

Are you developing the plans and people for the projects and teams that you lead?

Chapter 4 – Key Insights & Reflections

CHAPTER 5

"If your actions inspire others to dream more, learn more, do more and become more, you are a leader."
- John Quincy Adams

EXPOSED, EDUCATED, EMPOWERED

Will Smith tells a story about how his dad made him and his brother build a wall in front of the family business. It took them over a year to finish it, and when they started, they thought they'd never be able to do it. When the project was completed, Will's dad told the boys never to talk to him again about what they believed they couldn't do. According to Will, that one experience empowered him to believe in himself. Because his dad exposed him to a work ethic and process that taught him how to eliminate excuses and follow through on execution, Will was encouraged and empowered. The work ethic that his dad exposed him to as a child has stayed with him for life, and now he believes that anything is possible, regardless of what is going on around him.

Each and every day, leaders must expose themselves to information that will help them to grow so they can continue to encourage and empower the people who they are leading. Leaders can only take people as far as they themselves have gone, and the leader who refuses to keep learning will soon fail. Times and people change, and effective leaders are responsive to those changes. This is why leaders need multiple sources of encouragement from others - professionally, spiritually, and personally. To be able to give all that they give to educate, empower and encourage others, leaders must take time to refill their cups.

> Leaders expose themselves to information and experiences that will help them to grow so that the people they lead can grow.

The E's of Leadership

Leaders empower themselves and others by leading through example and executing with excellence.

Leaders educate and encourage themselves with positive examples so they will be empowered to lead more effectively without making excuses.

Leaders expose themselves to information and experiences that will help them to grow so the people they lead can grow.

Leaders are able to enlighten others as to what is truly possible.

Leaders require multiple sources of encouragement from other leaders - professionally, spiritually, and personally.

Leaders empower themselves with the skills and the will to empower others. Strong leaders know poor work ethic can easily undermine good talent.

Effective leaders execute the plan of action, while ineffective leaders give excuses for not executing.

Leaders understand they cannot put their energy and effort into people and projects that are emotionally draining.

Three things that I wish I would have known about leadership before I became a leader:

1. Expose yourself to positive people, places, and things.

2. Educate and enlighten yourself with the tools you need to lead.

3. Encourage yourself and others to execute with excellence.

Guiding Questions

Are you giving excuses for not executing or are you leading by example and executing with excellence?

How are you educating and empowering yourself with the skills and tools you need to be a better leader?

Chapter 5 – Key Insights & Reflections

CHAPTER 6

"Many people have commitment to the convenience. They'll stay faithful as long as it's safe and doesn't involve risk, rejection, or criticism." - Charles Stanley

FAITHFUL, FOCUSED, FRUITFUL

Nick Vujicic was born with no arms or legs, but he can do just about everything that a person with limbs can do. When he was a child, he knew that he was different. At age 10 he tried to commit suicide in the bathtub. He wasn't able to follow through, and when he came up from beneath the water, he came up with a vision. He realized how it would have affected his parents if he'd succeeded with his suicide attempt, and he realized that his life mattered. Even though he did things differently, he chose to have faith in his own unique journey.

When I saw Nick's interview on Oprah with Rick Warren, it changed my life. Nick said that you have to be "faithful to finish," and quitting on life is not an option. He talked about the days when he didn't feel like doing what needed to be done, but he chose to remain faithful to his course. Today Nick is married, has two degrees, and is living his dream of inspiring others all over the world.

> One of the most important things that leaders can do when things gets difficult is to focus on what they believe rather than what they're feeling in the moment.

Being faithful means having faith in our own capacity to keep going and do what needs to be done, even when the going gets difficult. It also means being faithful to our projects, our people, and ourselves. Leaders must be faithful in multiple areas to become fruitful. Being faithful can be difficult. It's demanding to summon the will to do what's needed when we don't feel like doing it, or to keep going when we're tired and not seeing the results of our efforts.

One of the most important things that leaders can do when things gets difficult is to focus on what they believe rather than what they're feeling in the moment. The will to prepare for the victory during practice is harder than playing in the game. When properly focused, faith can have a major positive impact on future endeavors.

The F's of Leadership

Effective leaders will share their flops, failures, flaws, and fumbles to teach others and encourage them to keep going.

When they begin a project, leaders must follow through to finish strong. This means being faithful to completing the task from the very beginning.

Strong commitment in the areas of faith, family, finance, and fitness will support leaders to be fruitful and to bring their vision to fruition.

Leaders remain faithful when the road is rough and results are not happening fast enough.

Leaders know how to focus on the future vision while they faithfully complete the tasks of the present moment.

Leaders know how to forgive, which means forgiving both

themselves and others for past and present shortcomings.

Leaders fruitfully produce positive results by staying faithful and focused.

Three things that I wish I would have known about leadership before I became a leader:

1. Focus on the future.

2. Always be faithful and follow through.

3. Forgive yourself and others when you fail, fall, flop, or fumble.

Guiding Questions

Are you faithful to the people you lead even when you're not seeing the fruits of your labors?

What are some areas where you can improve your focus?

Chapter 6 – Key Insights & Reflections

CHAPTER 7

"The unfortunate aspect about living life without your own goals is that you may very well reach a point in your life where you will wonder, 'what would have happened if I had only done _____.'"
- *Catherine Pulsifer*

GUTS, GROWTH, GIFTS

If you're going to be a leader, you must have the guts to stand up, stand out, and take charge. That's why leaders understand the importance of staying connected to a higher source for power, energy, and insight. Most leaders recognize the gift but sometimes they forget about the giver of the gift. I believe this is that sense of higher purpose, values, wisdom, and direction that keeps us doing the right things for the right reasons. Leaders must have the guts to lead and the guts to follow because they both work hand in hand. You must be willing and able to follow the vision and the values of your organization. When you are willing and able that means you have the ability and the attitude to lead. The world will continually offer distractions but you have the power to stay focus, and that same power also gives you the guts to do what you know is right even if everyone is questioning you.

In order for you to quit being great at being good and grow into being good at being great, it is essential to have that extra inspiration. Every day, you are growing and going forward, whether you are moving in a positive or negative direction. A leader must be careful not to wind up in the glow of the spotlight for the wrong reasons. Some leaders choose to grow into areas that may be very profitable financially, but don't support the wellbeing of their family and lifestyle.

> Leaders know that their gift will act as a compass, directing them toward their specific destiny.

Remember that it profits a man nothing to gain the whole world and lose his soul. What profit is there in growing a business and then not having anyone with whom to share it? Leaders must make sure they are constantly going, glowing, and growing in the right direction. Growth is the key to leading because when you are not growing as

a leader the people you lead will stop growing. One of the ways I grow personally, and I also share it with my family, is to have daily reminders of the following:
1. Always do what's right.
2. Always do your best.
3. Always do it for God.

We confess this twice a day to remind us of our value system as a family. I'm the first to admit that I haven't always succeeded in doing what's right, doing my best, or doing it for God. Sometimes it's hard to do what's right and what's best when others are not doing what's right and are giving half of the effort. I've learned as a leader and a follower to develop a compassion for the people, projects, and programs you're leading. You must also lead more with your actions instead of just leading with your words.

I believe everyone has a Gift which is described and defined as a natural ability or talent. Have you identified the gifts inside of the people you're leading? Have you identified the gift inside of yourself as a leader? Donald Trump, Tiger Woods, Lebron James, Bill Gates and the list goes on of people who lead in the area of their gifts. They dominate with their gift and it automatically positions them as a leader. What they do with the influence they have from the area of their gift where people follow them is up to them. Some people believe they don't need to develop their gift if it comes easy and naturally, but that is not true. Some people are born with a skill set that makes them effective leaders, but they still need to be developed. The reason why athletes say hard work can defeat talent when talent fails to work hard is because the hard work and consistent work ethic breeds courage and confidence. When leaders and the people they're leading are courageous and confident in their ability to use their gifts they will lead more effectively. It's imperative that leaders identify the gift in others and help cultivate it for growth.

The G's of Leadership

Leaders have the guts to both lead and be led, while always remaining grateful for the opportunity to lead.

Leaders realize staying connected will allow them to continue to grow, glow, and go from good to great.

Leaders are committed to the growth process in whatever areas they're leading.
Leaders understand the importance of cultiviating their power, energy and insight.

Leaders know the difference between what keeps them going and what keeps them growing.

Leaders have the guts to set a goal and stay the course until the goal has been reached.

Leaders believe in their gifts and the gifts of the people they're leading.

Leaders know that their gift will act as a compass, directing them toward their specific destiny.

Three things that I wish I would have known about leadership before I became a leader:

1. Keep going when you feel like quitting.

2. Keep glowing in the area of leadership where you shine the brightest.

3. Keep growing from good to great.

Guiding Questions

Where can you do more to encourage your greatest growth?

Are you connected to the higher source that empowers you to lead with the integrity and character you need to be effective?

Chapter 7 – Key Insights & Reflections

CHAPTER 8

"Life provides losses and heartbreak for all of us, but the greatest tragedy is to have the experience and miss the meaning. I am determined not to miss that meaning."
- Robin Roberts

HUMBLE, HOPEFUL, HEART-CENTERED

ABC Anchor Woman, Robin Roberts, is a TV personality known for inspiring millions. On the day that she announced she had breast cancer, hearts all over the world felt her pain. Throughout the process of chemotherapy and radiation and the physical and mental strain of those procedures, Robin kept up a positive spirit and a smile when she was on the air. She never stopped being an inspiration to others and she didn't let her hope or courage waver. When asked how she was doing, she declared, "I'm gonna beat this."

After about five years of being a cancer survivor, Robin was experiencing more professional success than ever before. She was also going through continued health challenges. On the same day that she received the honor of being called to interview President Obama, she underwent a very painful procedure to extract bone marrow for testing. Just a few weeks later, Robin reached a huge career milestone – for the first time in 16 years, Good Morning America beat the Today Show in ratings. At the height of her professional career, Robin was met with more difficult news. That very day, she received a diagnosis of Myelodysplastic Syndrome, a form of bone marrow cancer.

> Leaders use their hearts and heads to help hurting people heal.

The day Robin went public with her illness, the *Be the Match Registry*, a nonprofit run by the National Marrow Donor Program, had an 1,800% increase in donors. She took a leave from Good Morning America to get a bone marrow transplant, and was back after just 6 months. Robin received the 2012 Peabody Award for allowing her network to document her journey with a rare disease and build a public service campaign around it, raising awareness of the need for more donors and inspiring hundreds of potential donors to register. She also received the Arthur Ashe Courage Award in 2013, and finished out 2013 in good health, happiness, and success, both personally and professionally. Through all the pain of her illness and recovery, Robin Roberts was carried through by her ever-present hope.

Leaders realize even though they and the people they lead may be hurting, they must never stop hoping. This is because leaders understand the key to leading is HOPE. Hope is defined as "a feeling of expectation and desire for a certain thing to happen." Leaders know that to lead themselves and others through difficult times, they can call on HOPE :

Helping	Holding	Having
Other	Onto the	Only
People	Picture you're	Positive
Excel	Expecting	Expectations

When you hold onto the picture you're expecting, your hope becomes contagious. Through you, hope spreads to the people you are leading. Leaders know they can use hope to help others to excel during dark times, because hope always shines a light on what's possible.

In order to create lasting change, leaders must be willing to lead with both their hearts and their heads. Our heads help to make decisions, and our hearts keep us committed to those decisions and connected to the people who are affected by them. It's much easier when the heart and head are on the same page, and effective leaders look for solutions that can balance the two.

The habits of leaders must also be grounded in humility. This allows leaders to understand and have compassion for the people who they're leading. Humble leaders also have compassion for themselves, and know that when they are hurting, they can make the mistake of acting unconsciously in a way that also hurts others. My grandmother always said, "If you cannot help folks, then at least don't hurt them." Leaders understand that it's "HARD" to get through offenses when someone feels hurt. Sometimes avoiding hurting someone is not possible to do as a leader. Whether it's intentional or not, the role and the responsibility of a leader requires sharing information that may not always be welcomed by all. We may not have the power to control the information we receive as a leader but we do have the power to control how we respond. When someone hurts you I want you

HOPE
Helping Other People Excel

to remember one word to give you a strategy. Their was a time when as a leader I would experience hurt and the first emotion would be to get angry. Once anger settle in after hurt the next emotion drives people to get revenge. Revenge leads hurt people into trying to hurt people which normally leads to regrets and depression. When hurt leads to anger and revenge it causes people to become depressed.

Hurt	Hurt
Anger	Acknowledge
Revenge	Release
Depression	Delivered

Hurt is unavoidable at times so I encourage leaders to acknowledge the hurt. It's okay to inform yourself and others that something or someone hurt you. Effective leaders acknowledge what hurt them, when it hurt them, and move on without holding grudges and trying to get revenge. Once you acknowledge what hurt you it's easier to release the hurt and get delivered from it instead of depressed.

Leaders can hurt those they serve when they are operating out of fear or doubt. Anytime an action or decision is born from a place of unforgiveness or regret or is motivated by selfish gains, then fear is in the driver's seat. A humble leader who operates with heart and hope can always expect the best.

The H's of Leadership

Leaders have positive habits that bring forth positive changes. Leaders are humble and shouldn't become arrogant as they lead.

In order to understand and have compassion for the people they lead, a leader's habits must be grounded in humility.

Leaders use their hearts and heads to help hurting people heal.

Leaders are able to hear the hearts of the people they lead, and this is how they know the best path to follow.

Leader's heads help them to think about what people need, and their hearts help them to feel what others need.

Leaders keep hoping for the best, even under the worst circumstances.

Leaders use their heads to make decisions, but their hearts keep them committed to those decisions.

Leaders are willing to lead with both their hearts and their heads to create change.

Leaders understand they may be hated for some of the things they do and the decisions they make.

A heart-centered leader is able to bring hope to the hearts of others, and in this way brings out the best in all.

Three things that I wish I would have known about leadership before I became a leader:

1. Allow past hurts and hang ups to heal so that you won't be hindered.

2. In the face of pain and problems keep hoping instead of hurting.

3. Use your heart, your head, and your hands to help you.

Guiding Questions

Are you hurting and losing hope because of your present circumstances?

How can you lead with both your head and your heart?

Chapter 8 – Key Insights & Reflections

CHAPTER 9

"How do you expect to get a return on life when you've never invested in living."
- Mansfield Key III

INVEST, IMPACT, INSPIRE

In 1965, a gentleman by the name of Fred Deluca was on his way to fulfilling his dream of becoming a medical doctor. He was looking for a way to pay for his education, and a family friend suggested that he open a submarine sandwich shop. Fred received a $1,000 investment loan from another friend, Dr. Peter Buck, who also became Fred's partner. Together, they opened their first store in Bridgeport, Connecticut in August of 1965. The two friends set a goal to open 32 stores in 10 years. In 1974 they realized they couldn't meet that goal on their own, so they began franchising.

Today, Subway has over 40,000 stores worldwide and is one of the most successful franchises in the world. One man's investment influenced a doctor who then went on to impact the world and inspire millions. The impact of that initial investment extended beyond what either of them had ever imagined to be possible.

Leaders will be called to invest time and money in people, places, and projects. This investment is a leader's way of serving others. When leaders invest in other people, it gives them an opportunity to influence them. When leaders invest in and influence other people, they will also impact those people's lives. Through their patience and passion, leaders can inspire others to accomplish what appears to be impossible at the time.

To inspire others, leaders must be committed to igniting growth in both themselves and others. Leaders strike the match, light the candle, and then pass the torch. In the words of James Heller, "a candle loses nothing by lighting another candle."

> Good leaders imagine the impossible as possible and use influence to get others to believe in what they see.

The I's of Leadership

Leaders are actively involved in igniting the process of growth, starting with themselves and then inspiring others.

Leaders identify potential problems and possibilities before they arise, then immediately discern what's needed.

Leaders invest time and money in themselves, people, and programs as a means of serving others.

As leaders invest in and influence others, it impacts the lives of both the leader and the follower.

A leader inspires and brings hope to others by overcoming challenges and accomplishing goals.

Leaders inspire others to want to accomplish more.

Leaders investigate the path and lead with confidence through uncharted territory.

Good leaders imagine the impossible as possible and use influence to get others to believe in what they see.

Leaders seek to see a person's internal potential regardless of what may be showing on the outside.

Three things that I wish I would have known about leadership before I became a leader:

1. It's important to properly invest time and money in yourself and others.

2. As a leader, you can use your influence to positively inspire and impact others.

3. Follow your instincts to make the best decisions in the moment.

Guiding Questions

Are you positively influencing the people you lead, or are you allowing yourself to be influenced?

Can you imagine the impossible happening in your life?

Chapter 9 – Key Insights & Reflections

"Life is a journey that must be traveled, no matter how bad the roads and accommodations."
- Oliver Goldsmith

JOURNALING, JOINABLE, JOYFUL

Strong and successful leaders know how to learn from their mistakes and the mistakes of others. Keeping a journal of the past and present is an important habit, because it creates a record of mistakes, strategies, insights, and solutions. Journaling past failures can lead to future successes. We're able to overcome past pitfalls and mistakes as we gain experience, and we gain experience by making mistakes. The people who choose to learn from their mistakes are the ones who grow into great leaders. By journaling their journeys, leaders leave footprints for others to follow.

Effective leaders can juggle multiple tasks as they lead, and they also know not to make the mistake of taking on too many tasks at once and then dropping the ball. There's no use in being a jack of all trades and a master of none. Leaders also know how to clearly justify and explain their actions, including the delegation of responsibilities, because they have analyzed the potential consequences beforehand.

To be joinable, leaders must be able to generate excitement around their cause or vision. By leading from a place of joy, leaders inspire others to want to join them. Jesus was a leader dedicated to serving others, and he lived an example from which all leaders can learn. Jesus led and the people followed for multiple reasons. Some people followed because of what they believed Jesus could do for them, and others followed because they wanted to serve and support such a great leader.

Of the many examples of Jesus' leadership principles, one of the greatest is when he saw his soon-to-be disciples Peter and Andrew casting their nets into the ocean. Jesus told them that if they followed him, he would make them fishers of men. He took ordinary men with skills and expertise in a certain area and exposed them to his works. He educated, encouraged, and empowered them to do greater works.

Although Jesus lead thousands, he only taught 12 disciples. His leadership was not based on numbers. He only lived 33 years, so his leadership was not based on a long life of influence and service. The effectiveness of Jesus' leadership was and is founded on the strength of the example that he left for others to follow, in his life and in his death.

> Leaders journal both past and present experiences to track mistakes, strategies, solutions and successes.

He was the ultimate follower because he only did what his father said to do. He was the ultimate leader because the strongest message was his walk and not just his words. He showed leaders you can never out preach or out teach the life you live. Thankfully his journey was journaled for people to live by even today. Is your journey as a leader being journaled for future leaders to follow?

The J's of Leadership

Happiness is born of good things happening, but joy is constant regardless of circumstances. A balanced leader can remain joyful through all the ups and downs of the journey.

Leaders inspire others to want to join them by living and leading joyfully.

Leaders are able to juggle multiple projects as they lead.

Leaders must be aware of when they are juggling too many tasks and their primary focus begins to suffer.

Leaders can justify their actions and decisions to others who may not agree or understand, and they know how to judge and weigh the consequences beforehand.

Leaders should journal often on their journey, making note of the road and route to success.

Leaders journal both past and present experiences to track mistakes, strategies, solutions and successes.

Leaders also journal their future plans: "Write the vision and make it plain so the people can follow it."

Three things that I wish I would have known about leadership before I became a leader:

1. Journaling is an important way of leaving a path for others to follow.

2. Being joyful inspires people to join your cause.

3. The leadership principles of Jesus and the journal he left behind are great guides for any leader.

Guiding Questions

Are you juggling too many tasks and allowing your primary focus to suffer?

Do you know how to lead with joy so others will join you?

How could you better integrate some of Jesus' leadership principles into your own?

Chapter 10 – Key Insights & Reflections

CHAPTER 11

"To know what you know and what you do not know, that is true knowledge." - Confucius

KNOWLEDGE, KINDNESS, KNOW-HOW

A good friend of mine likes to say that "The key to life is being in the right place at the right time doing the right thing with the right people in the right way. You'll be guaranteed to succeed." He followed that statement by explaining that he fell into trouble when he was in the wrong place at the wrong time doing the wrong thing with the wrong people. This personal motto was his key to leadership. What is your personal key?

To be a leader, you have to know and understand your personal key. A key is a tool or technique that helps a person to unlock the doorways to opportunity, ability, and potential. Once leaders understand and appreciate what is unique about them, they will become confident in their own distinct leadership style and skills and know what key to use and when to use it. These defining characteristics are a leader's KEYS to Knowledge, and know-how is understanding how to apply these keys to everyday situations.

> Leaders understand that what makes the biggest difference is not what you know, but what you do with what you know.

Everyone has a gift, talent, and ability that is unique to them. Often, it's a leader's role to help others to identify their own unique abilities and gifts. Good leaders support the people who they lead by empowering and encouraging them to develop the key skills and abilities that help not only the company or the project, but also the individual.

Many leaders have cultivated their ability to recognize the doorway of opportunity and identify the key that will open it. For instance, if the lock that is holding people in poverty is ignorance, then leaders recognize that the key to unlock the door is education. The key that motivates one employee to perform can cause another employee to shut down. The same motivation that inspires one volunteer to action may offend or upset another. Different situations require different leadership styles. One style may be great for leading a group of people, while another may be more effective for leading a project or implementing a new program. By learning to adapt your leadership style to the situation, you can more effectively and efficiently achieve the goals and objectives at hands.

When you understand your own unique keys and know how to look for the keys in others, you are able to lead with kindness. As a leader, you must be kind to yourself by knowing your own skills, gifts, and limitations, and by knowing what to ask of yourself and what not to ask of yourself. The same goes for the people who you lead. Looking on others with a kind eye means being able to see them where they are, and know where and when to push and when not to push. When you exhibit kindness in your actions toward others, more and more people will be attracted to your vision.

The K's of Leadership

Leaders are kind and approachable, not arrogant.

Leaders are equipped with the knowledge, kindness, and know-how necessary to lead others.

Leaders understand what makes the biggest difference is not what you know, but what you do with what you know.

Leaders have a keen mindset that allows them to lead themselves and others into unknown territory.

Leaders must possess the keys that help to unlock the potential in the people who they lead.

Leaders are knowledgeable in the area in which they have chosen to lead.

Leaders have know-how, which means they are skilled at applying the knowledge they've acquired to everyday situations.

Effective leaders understand they don't need to know all the answers to every question if they know who to ask or how to access the answers.

Intelligent leaders know a key can open or lock a door. Keys that unlock potential can be the difference in leaders opening the doors of opportunity or getting locked out of opportunity.

A leader's ability to see the door of opportunity and recognize what key will open it can make all the difference.

Three things that I wish I would have known about leadership before I became a leader:

1. Identify your personal leadership key and style.

2. Identify what you need to do to cultivate those personal keys.

3. Know how to identify the keys that are needed and when to use them.

Guiding Questions

What has been your personal key to unlocking opportunity and potential? What is your own specific key and leadership style?

What happens when you lead without understanding the KEYs to Leadership?

Chapter 11 – Key Insights & Reflections

"One of the most sincere forms of respect is actually listening to what another has to say."
- Bryant H. McGill

LOOKING, LISTENING, LEARNING

There's an old story about a woman who insisted on taking her husband to the doctor because she thought he'd gone deaf and she was tired of talking to him without getting any response. She called her local physician and told him she needed to bring her husband in to get his hearing tested. The doctor asked, "Where is he now?" The woman told the doctor that her husband was underneath the car, doing some repair work. The doctor explained there was something that he needed her to try before she brought her husband into the office. He told the woman, "Go outside and ask your husband a question from a distance and see if he responds. Then, if he doesn't answer, go stand about five feet away from him and ask the same question again. If that still doesn't work, get right next to the car and ask the question one more time. If he still doesn't answer, then you can bring him in." After hanging up the phone, the woman walked to the garage door and called outside, "Bobby, what do you want for dinner?" She didn't hear anything, so she walked to about five feet away from the car and asked the same question. She didn't hear anything. She took the last few steps over to the car and then, as loudly as she could, shouted, "Bobby, what do you want for dinner?!" Bobby slid out from underneath the car, looked her in the eyes and said, "Woman, I've told you three times that I've already eaten!"

The moral of the story is simple. Leaders may believe that the people they lead aren't listening, but the truth is leaders are the ones who need to listen. Parents can blame their children for not listening, but how often do parents remember to really listen to their children? Leaders must make a conscious decision to listen to the concerns of the people they lead, and to acknowledge their perspectives as valid and important.

In order to continue to lead effectively, leaders must closely look at and observe the people they lead, the services they provide, and the products they deliver. Leaders must also listen to and receive feedback from their customers, clients, and/or constituents about their leadership style.

By developing a keen eye and ear and working to look and listen to the feedback you're receiving from your environment, you set yourself up to do the single most important thing a leader has to do all of the time: learning. If you want to know what your next steps need to be, look to and learn from your surroundings. If you want to know what new skills and strengths you need to cultivate, listen to and learn from the feedback you're getting. The moment right in front of you is always your greatest teacher.

> Leaders must closely look at and observe the people they lead, the services they provide, and the products they deliver.

People like to work with a person with whom they can laugh. It doesn't mean that you have to tell jokes and be cheerful to lead, but it does help to build good relationships. Being likable and laughable makes you approachable.

It's important to know the right times for humor and the right times for seriousness. While leadership is definitely not a popularity contest, it's important for employees to enjoy your company and the atmosphere of their work environment. A big part of this atmosphere is determined by how the leader reacts to concerns regarding their product or service.

The L's of Leadership

Leaders must be able to limit negative thoughts and people who are nonproductive and toxic.

Leaders cannot be liars and expect others to think they are trustworthy. Lying will prevent leaders from connecting once the truth is revealed.

Remember to look, listen, laugh, and learn before leading.

Leaders know that if they want to build loyalty, they must respect the people they work for, the people they work with, and the products or services they're providing.

Effective leaders are able to look at and observe the people who they lead, the services they provide, and the products they deliver.

Leaders listen to their customers, clients, and/or constituents about the effectiveness of their leadership style.

Leaders are always learning new skills, techniques, and life lessons to increase their effectiveness as leaders.

Leaders look at and listen to a variety of sources and learn from them before making decisions.

Leaders know how to have and create laughable moments.

People want to work with and for leaders who are likable.

Leaders are always open to learning from the people they lead.

Leaders cannot be lazy and expect to be successful.

Leaders limit the negative intake from their mental diets. What goes in is what comes out.

Leaders have access to sensitive information, and they must use integrity and good moral judgment about sharing information.

Leaders must not seek to become likable at the risk of losing influence, authority, and the respect of those they lead.

Leaders use their losses to learn how to become winners.

Three things that I wish I would have known about leadership before I became a leader:

1. Looking and listening to others will help you learn as a leader.
2. Losing can lead to winning when you learn from the loss.
3. Leaders don't have to be likable or humorous to lead… but it can really help!

Guiding Questions

Look and observe your own leadership style. What are you doing that's effective? What is ineffective?

Do your efforts to be likable belittle your authority and power to lead? Or do you need to work on making yourself more likable and approachable?

How often do you focus on listening, learning, and laughing with the people you lead? How can you focus on this area more?

Chapter 12 – Key Insights & Reflections

CHAPTER 13

"Motives reveal why we do what we do, which is actually more important to God than what we're doing."
- Joyce Meyer

METHODS, MOTIVES, MISSION

Leaders understand the importance of using modern methods to problem solve. Today's workforce is constantly changing. The expectation that people will commit their entire career to one company is a thing of the past, unless it happens to be their own company. A hierarchical, top down approach will lead to high turnovers and poor employee performance. Leaders are not required to justify every decision, but they do need to give employees a clear understanding of what is being asked of them and why.

Employees want to know what the mission is so they can know their motivation. Knowing this is what supports employees in trusting their leader's judgment and motives. That's good management, plain and simple. This helps individuals to buy into the process and care about the success of the project and/or the company. Creating this kind of work environment will help leaders to maximize every opportunity to further the company's mission. When leaders themselves are motivated by the mission, they will maximize each moment on the journey.

A leader's vision is different from a leader's mission. The vision is the long-term goal shared by leaders and their team. The mission is the path of action and implementation taken to reach that goal. While the vision clearly defines the larger goals, values, and purpose that inspire everyone to move forward, the mission defines specifics: what are we doing, who's doing it, and how?

The mission articulates, step by step, the path to carrying out the vision. To be an effective leader, you must be motivated by the mission, not just the vision. To be motivated by the mission means you are motivated by the work that helps you and your team to reach the goals of the vision. For instance, if the vision is to be #1 in quality service providing the best computer repair in the city, the mission is to do the repair work and provide the service. This involves training in the latest technology to stay cutting edge and relevant; going above and beyond to serve the customer even when you don't feel like it; maintaining a "customer is always right" policy even when you know sometimes they're wrong. All of these things can become frustrating if a leader loses sight of the vision. The vision guides the mission; the mission carries out the vision.

The key for leaders is to be motivated by their mission and to understand the methods that work for their particular field. These two things determine leadership style. There are 3 key steps to completing any task: understand the MISSION; use the right METHODS; and have the right MOTIVES. The methods that a leader would use to motivate some people wouldn't be effective with others. The coach who leads a team to the Super Bowl championship may not be as effective in a corporate setting. You would lead your sales team differently from the way you'd lead your family. Every field, from a local prison to small business to church, requires a special type of leadership.

Whatever field you've chosen to lead, make sure

> Leaders know it is mandatory to proceed with pure motives and a clear mission.

that you're using the right methods of motivation. With a clear cut mission, any task becomes attainable because you know the methods and steps required to fulfill your vision. When people are following a leader who lacks a clear mission, frustration is inevitable. But when the vision and the mission are clear, people will connect with it even if they're not closely connected to the leader. This is why weak or unskilled leaders with vision are sometime considered to be better than skilled, experienced leaders with no vision. Even if the leader is weak, a clear and inspiring vision can attract strong people with quality skills.

The M's of Leadership

Leaders are able to measure progress to determine the effectiveness of the project and the people they're leading.

Leaders are able to maximize the moment and provide meaning and understanding during times of difficulty.

Leaders are mentors to others and also need to be mentored by others.

Mentors can give leaders the shortcuts. Leaders without mentors will take the long route.

Leaders understand the importance of using modern methods and approaches in their work.

Leaders know it is mandatory to proceed with pure motives and a clear mission.

When leaders operate from the right motivations, it improves the performance of everyone around them.

The first step effective leaders take is to check in with the mission and search their hearts to make sure it's aligned with their personal motives.

A leader who is truly motivated by passion and purpose for the mission has the greatest power to influence others.

Through understanding the mission, leaders know how to put the method of operation into action.

Leaders know that their vision must be created mentally before it can be manifested physically and materially.

Leaders must be able to learn from their own mistakes and, even more importantly, learn from the mistakes of others.

Leaders must sense the potentials of the moment to capitalize on the opportunity to make a difference and money while changing lives.

Effective leaders don't only motivate, but they mobilize and monetize every possible moment for the benefits of the mission.

Three things that I wish I would have known about leadership before I became a leader:

1. Always check your motivation first.

2. Maximize potentials by using the most modern methods and approaches available.

3. Your genuine passion for the mission is the biggest motivator for the people you lead.

Guiding Questions

What is your motivation?

What is your mission statement?

Have you ever led a mission that was not aligned with your motives, or have you ever led from the wrong motivation?

What were the consequences of your choice(s)?

Chapter 13 – Key Insights & Reflections

CHAPTER 14

"If I cannot navigate thru the obstacle course of purpose and negotiate with the one who has the prize, then I will never receive the promise."
- Mansfield Key III

NETWORK, NAVIGATE, NEGOTIATE

Leaders understand the power and necessity of networking, because they know success requires connection. While some people are natural networkers, with a personality and skillset that makes them readily attractive to others, some are more like social caterpillars than social butterflies. I struggled tremendously in this area, and I found myself shying away from places and people that were vital connections for me on my path to leadership success.

I knew that to succeed, I needed to learn to network, and so I did. What I learned first is the key to networking is knowing that people like to feel special – people love to talk about themselves and what they do, and they also love to share about what and who they know. When I learned to put my personal agenda on the backburner and started listening to others and making them the priority, my networking skills improved dramatically. I also learned the 3 C's of networking, navigating, and negotiating:

1. Connect with people right where they are, the way they are.
2. Create the link between what they need and the service or product you provide.
3. Close the deal and provide the product and/or service in a way that excels and exceeds their expectations.

Marketing gurus have determined that the strongest advertising is word of mouth. Your network determines your net worth, so as a leader you must learn to capitalize on your connections. Today, however, the span of a network is far wider than it has ever been before, which makes it even more essential for business. In the past, word of mouth was passed through you or someone else recommending your product or service. Today, however, we use social media and the extended social networks to share by word of mouth what we are offering and the benefits that it provides. As a leader, you must adapt and adjust to the tools available in order to network, navigate, and negotiate with the greatest success.

> Leaders know how to negotiate and navigate with a nimble mind.

The N's of Leadership

Leaders are able to measure progress to determine the effectiveness of the project and the people they're leading.

Leaders are able to maximize the moment and provide meaning and understanding during times of difficulty.

Leaders are mentors to others and also need to be mentored.

Mentors can provide shortcuts for leaders. Leaders without mentors will take the long and difficult route.

Leaders understand the importance of using modern methods and approaches in their work.

Leaders know it is mandatory to proceed with pure motives and a clear mission.

When leaders operate with the right motivations, it improves the performance of everyone around them.

The first step effective leaders take is to check in with the mission and search their hearts to make sure it's aligned with their personal motives.

Through understanding the mission, leaders know how to put the method of operation into action.

Three things that I wish I would have known about leadership before I became a leader:

1. Naysayers can be your greatest motivators.

2. Navigate from what you know to be best for everyone involved.

3. Never hesitate or procrastinate on making necessary decisions.

Guiding Questions

What can you do to improve your networking skills?

How can you turn the voices of naysayers, both outer and inner, into motivators?

How do you make room for negotiation, in your business or in your personal life? Do you know how to create win-win situations?

Chapter 14 – Key Insights & Reflections

CHAPTER 15

"You will never get the right Outcome in your life, with the wrong Outlook on your life."
- Mansfield Key III

OPTIONS, OUTLETS, OPPORTUNITIES

Leaders are able to see options, outlets, and opportunities in every situation. The only thing that success guarantees is yet another opportunity to fail. Oftentimes, we see the outward success that an individual has attained, but never get to see the countless obstacles that they had to overcome to reach success. I am often reminded of the scene in the televison show "Fame" where Debbie Allen is giving her infamous speech to the new group of dancers.

She says, "You want to be famous? Well, fame costs, and right here is where you start paying in blood, sweat and tears."

As leaders, most of us understand we have to put in the work, and putting in the work means being willing to transform obstacles into opportunities. As I like to say, "No doesn't necessarily mean no, it simply means not yet."

So, what are the steps to transforming obstacles into opportunity? First, when presented with an obstacle, take a step back and survey your options. Options are the positive and empowering choices that you can make when it seems life is only showing you opposition. Once you've surveyed your options, then identify your outlets. Outlets are the openings that reveal your pathway of growth through the present obstacles. By following these outlets, you arrive at opportunities, which are the chances, choices, lessons, and good fortune that you've created out of bad luck, misfortune, and hard times. To summarize, the path from obstacle to opportunity can be broken down into three steps:

1. When faced with an obstacle, survey your options.
2. After looking at your options, identify your outlets.

3. Follow the outlet to opportunity's doorstep…
   and don't forget to knock!

There's no question that it's essential for leaders to pursue opportunity. However, a major pitfall on the path to opportunity is in overvaluing the opinions of others. We've all made the mistake of valuing someone else's opinion above and beyond what we know to be right.

Once, when I was giving a speech before a church congregation with thousands of members, I almost changed everything I had planned because I wanted a very well-known Bishop who was there in the audience to like me. I was so nervous about making a good impression that I was trembling, and the leader of the ministry that I was involved with noticed and came over to talk to me before I went up to speak. He said, "You're worried about the wrong thing right now. You have a God-given gift to share with the world, and you're worried about the opinions of one man. Look at all those people out there who need what you have! You will never become successful if you're always worried about the opinions of a few people."

> **Ineffective leaders see only obstacles, opponents, and oppositions, and fail to see how they can overcome them to create the optimal outcome.**

Even though I knew that he was right, I was still curious to know what the Bishop thought. Long story short, once I'd completed my speech I received some valuable feedback – the Bishop had gotten an emergency call right before I went up to speak, so he didn't see or hear any of it. I had almost changed everything I was doing to impress the one person who wasn't even in the room.

The lesson that I learned was clear as daylight – when it comes to the work that you were placed in this world to do, don't mind the opinions of others. Of course, everyone wants to be validated, appreciated, and celebrated for something. I'm not saying that the opinions of others don't matter, but as a leader you can't allow what others think to be the measuring stick for your actions and accomplishments. You will face days full of complaint, controversy, criticism, conflict, and no compliments. This is why leaders must be able to live and decide above the opinions of others, whether those opinions are good or bad. Whatever others might be saying, only you can know if you're giving the best you have to offer, and that's the only true measuring stick of success.

The O's of Leadership

Leaders are not swayed by the opinions of others.

Leaders are open to change and are not easily offended.

Ineffective leaders see only obstacles, opponents, and oppositions, and fail to see how they can overcome obstacles to create the optimal outcome.

All leaders are faced with obstacles and opposition, but successful leaders are able to identify their options and opportunities.

Effective leaders accept constructive feedback, but they do not live, lead, or make decisions based on the opinions of others.

When leaders are open to suggestions, chances are they will make the optimal decision for everyone involved.

Leaders understand the difference that can be made by the power of one.

Leaders don't take offense at criticism because they know how to use it to meet their objectives more efficiently.

Three things that I wish I would have known about leadership before I became a leader:

1. See options instead of opponents.

2. See outlets instead of opposition.

3. Don't let your actions or decisions be swayed by the opinions of others.

Guiding Questions

How can you create options, outlets, and opportunities from your present obstacles, opponents, and opposition?

Are there any areas where you're not doing what you know to be right out of concern over the opinions of others?

Chapter 15 – Key Insights & Reflections

"Once you identify purpose it will give you the power to push and pursue your full potential."
- Mansfield Key III

PERSISTENCE, PLANNING, POSITIVITY

I remember the day I was forced to leave my job. I loved my job as Director and Founder of the FAMILY Program for a Head Start program, but I was being called to speak and travel more and more. I had started to take personal days and unpaid time off so that I could fulfill my speaking engagements. On August 13, 2007, I was called to make a decision before the Board of Education. I had requested a one year leave of absence so that I could pursue my speaking career, and even though I already knew that I would choose a career as a speaker over my current job, I still wanted a safety net to fall back on in case speaking didn't work out. The members of the Board told me I was no exception to the rules and they wouldn't grant me the leave, but said they would give me a few days to think it over and make my decision.

I left the office that Monday evening feeling deeply torn about what I wanted my next step to be. The next day, I received an email offering three options: report back to work immediately; turn in a written resignation by 1:30 pm; or be terminated from my position. I had worked so hard to build the FAMILY Program, and I was deeply upset at being forced out of my position. However, that moment forced me to see the truth. I was about to make a decision that would change the rest of my life.

I had always pictured myself as a successful speaker. Even though I had complained about the job at the FAMILY Program holding me back and not paying enough, I was still afraid to jump. What if my business as a speaker wasn't successful? What if leaving this job sent my family into poverty? Should I go back to work and leave next year after I'd saved up more money, or should I step out on faith? These were the questions running through my head as the clock ticked closer and closer to 1:30. I realized I was wanting the reward without the risk and the pay without the pressure. I gave my resignation that day, because the mental picture that I saw inspired me to perform under the pressure.

Even though being forced to resign from my position at the FAMILY Program felt like a high price to pay at the time, I chose to maintain a positive attitude and capitalize on the situation. Losing that job gave me a chance to focus on my plan of action, my speaking career and start making the most of my speaking opportunities. Sometimes, it's the pressure, the pain, and the persecution in the process that lead you to peace, purpose, and the position of power.

> Sometimes, it's the pressure, the pain, and the persecution in the process that lead you to peace, purpose, and the position of power.

The moral of this story is good leaders use positivity, persistence, and planning to create opportunities, and ineffective leaders complain about the process. Until the destination is chosen and planned, there's no way to know whether or not we've arrived, nor is there any way to effectively prepare and pursue the plan. When leaders prepare to pursue their plan, they place themselves in a position to capitalize on opportunities.

Leaders must be able to see the bigger picture, lay out

the plan, and prepare themselves and others to pursue it with persistence and positivity. When leaders can see the big picture that means they have a vision. When there's a vision, it's possible to construct a blueprint, even if the step-by-step process isn't completely clear. Sometimes, the dream is so far-reaching that it has to be processed in stages. The most effective leaders know this when they create the plan, so they prepare with patience, follow through with persistence, and use positivity as the glue that holds the project together when the going gets rough.

The P's of Leadership

Leaders are willing to pay the price that it takes to lead.

Leaders maintain a positive attitude in their approach to people, programs, and projects.

Leaders are able to rise above politics.

Leaders cannot sacrifice their purpose or vision of the big picture for the sake of popularity.

Strong leaders are more concerned about private integrity

than they are about public image.

Leaders know how to see the bigger picture, lay out the plan, and pursue it with patience and positivity.

Picturing, planning, preparing, and pursuing are essential actions for leaders. Avoiding any of these will result in problems, pain, and procrastination.

Leaders can create a plan of action to guide others through any process and project, no matter how big or how small.

Leaders can picture themselves and the people they are leading beyond their current situations.

Ineffective leaders see the problems, complain about the process, and get stuck in their pain. Instead of pursuing their plans, they procrastinate.

Leaders must be willing to patiently handle the pressures of deadlines and program requirements.

Leaders are willing to persistently push toward the prize.

Leaders understand they have the power to predict a

portion of the future, because what they choose to pursue today can produce what they desire for tomorrow. Leaders see possibilities when others see problems.

Leaders understand there is a direct connection between finding passion and purpose and reaching full potential.

Leaders are able to harness their passion, purpose, and pace themselves to place themselves in a better position.

Effective leaders know how to perform under pressure.

Effective leaders maintain peak performance by knowing when to push the team and when to pull back.

Effective leaders can allow their plan and process to be challenged without feeling they're being challenged as a person.

A "boss" or "manager" leads because of position and title, but leaders lead because they've made the people their priority.

Three things that I wish I would have known about leadership before I became a leader:

1. Picturing the vision will give you fuel to pursue the vision.

2. "Paying the price" of leadership requires patience and persistence.

3. Great possibilities can be produced out of pressure and problems.

Guiding Questions

In what areas do you tend to procrastinate – is it seeing the picture, laying out the plan, or preparing and pursuing?

As a leader, are you able to stay positive and persist when projects don't go as planned?

Chapter 16 – Key Insights & Reflections

CHAPTER 17

"The quality of your life is in the quality of your relationships." - Anthony Robbins

QUALITY, QUALIFICATIONS, QUINTESSENCE

Olympic gold medalist Gabby Douglas and her family went above and beyond to get to the Olympics. The Douglas family almost went bankrupt trying to fund Gabby's training (and she had to live in a different state to work with her coach.) Being away from her family was challenging for Gabby, and while she was in training for the qualifying meet she decided she wanted to quit. She said that it was all too much and she wanted to go back home and live a normal life. The sacrifice seemed too great, and quitting looked like the only option.

The sacrifice was great, but there was an even greater purpose behind the price that was being paid. Thankfully, Gabby's mother, her family, and her coach convinced her to complete her training and go to the qualifying meet. The rest is history. Gabby became the first woman from the U.S. to win both a team and an individual Olympic gold medal in the same year, as well as being the first African-American woman to win the all-around.

> Leaders understand that effective communication comes through the quality of their words, not the quantity of their words.

On any path of leadership, qualms will arise. There will be moments of anxiety and uncertainty or self-doubt, and quitting will seem like the easiest way out. Leaders know that they must be able to persevere and follow-through, even when they feel like quitting. They also know that in those challenging moments, its quality relationships that help them to stay the course. Without the continued encouragement or support of her family, Gabby would never have gone on to win the Olympic gold. Whether the endeavor is personal or professional, relationships are always the key to success.

The relationship can be with an acquaintance, a

business contact, a family member, or a friend, but the best foundation is always the same. I once heard a man say that quality relationships are built on truth, trust, and transparency. Trust is built with time and the knowledge that someone can be trusted to do what they've said they'll do when they said they would do it. The best way to build trust is to work at being trustworthy. We start building quality relationships through leading by example, by being willing to exemplify the qualities that we ourselves want in a relationship. When leaders are truthful and transparent with the people who they lead, it also builds a better rapport.

Leaders are guided by a sense of greater purpose, and certain relationships will pull them away from that purpose. Conversely, that purpose will also guide them away from certain relationships. I've always said that "our worst days with the right people are still better than our best days with the wrong ones." The road to great relationships can get rough sometimes, but leaders don't quit on their relationships unless they know that those relationships are not supporting their greater purpose. In order to reach your full potential on your path to leadership, you must identify the relationships that you need to begin, as well as relationships that you need to end.

The quintessence of leadership also has to do with

relationships. One of the most essential qualities of leaders is their capacity to call forth the best in the people around them, and to continue to call forth the best in themselves. In the presence of a quintessential leader, people feel empowered and inspired to become more of who they are and bring more of their gifts into the world.

By being trustworthy and empowering others, leaders are able to magnetize quality and qualified people to work with them. As leaders continue to grow and build their own qualifications, they train others, and pass those qualifications on. When you work or mentor closely with a true leader, you become qualified to be a leader yourself.

The Q's of Leadership

Leaders are able to inspire people who are on the verge of quitting.

Leaders seek quality relationships on their life's quest.

Leaders know how to attract and sustain relationships with quality allies, supporters, and colleagues.

Qualms are uneasy feelings of doubt and uncertainty, and

when leaders are having qualms about themselves or their path, they pass it on to the people who they lead.
Leaders create quality relationships, both personally and professionally, that will enhance their lives.

Leaders understand effective communication comes through the quality of their words, not the quantity of their words.

Successful leaders are able to keep going past the point when they want to quit.

Leaders lead effectively not because they know all the right answers, but because they ask the right questions.

A quintessential leader maintains a high standard for self and others, and always empowers and inspires others to be their best.

Three things that I wish I would have known about leadership before I became a leader:

1. Always seek quality relationships.

2. Feeling qualms and moving through it is part of the growth process.

3. Never quit until the task is complete.

Guiding Questions

Are your current relationships helping or hindering your personal or professional progress?

What is the quintessence of your personal leadership style? How do you empower and inspire others?

Chapter 17 – Key Insights & Reflections

CHAPTER 18

"True leaders understand they must be relatable, reliable, relevant, and real."
- Mansfield Key III

RELATABLE, RELIABLE, REAL

Leaders must be willing to be relatable so the people they lead can connect with them. They also need to be willing to be a reliable resource so that people can learn to trust them. The best way to build a reputation of being relatable and reliable is to lead in a way that is genuine, authentic, and real.

Abraham Lincoln once said, "Character is like a tree and reputation like its shadow. The shadow is what we think of it; the tree is the real thing." What's also true is that a person's reputation, the "shadow" cast by their character, really does precede them. I have had the honor of meeting many famous individuals over the years, and I often thought that I had a good idea of what they would be like based on their reputations. What I came to realize was I was looking at their shadows, which are often distortions of what's really there. Imagine walking into a darkened room and trying to discern what's there, and then turning on the light to find things completely different.

> Leaders know that they can lead more effectively by relating with others than by controlling others.

Leaders should be able to shine a light through the shadows to reveal a person's true character. When leaders have the capacity to recognize a person's true character, they can effectively review and resolve conflicts when problems arise. This also means leaders should try to see a person's full potential, even if that person isn't living up to it quite yet. By relating to a person based on where they are while maintaining a vision of what they can be, leaders inspire and empower the growth of the people they're leading.

The R's of Leadership

Leaders understand the importance of recognizing and rewarding the people they lead.

Leaders know how to receive criticism and grow from it, so it makes them better, not bitter.

Leaders choose to release regrets quickly so that they can move forward.

Leaders relate to the latest trends and technology in order to stay relevant.

Leaders are real and authentic when engaging with others.

By relating to people where they are, the way they are, leaders are able to help lead others to where they are destined to go.

When problems arise, leaders know how to react, respond, and rebound from setbacks.

When leaders recover from past hurts, habits, and hang-ups, they can recommit to being productive.

Leaders are a reliable resource of information and inspiration for the people they lead.

Leaders know how to be real in their expression of who they are and what they expect from others.

Leaders understand the power of their revenue and resources comes through the right relationships.

Effective leaders know how to reflect, review, and resolve conflict.

Leaders know they can lead more effectively by relating with others than by controlling others.

Three things that I wish I would have known about leadership before I became a leader:

1. Always find the common ground from which to relate to others.

2. Know the difference between reacting and responding.

3. In the face of setbacks and losses, choose to release regrets and regroup for success.

Guiding Questions

What area in your life do you need to release regrets so that you can move forward?

Are you able to see a person's real character, or do you get stuck on reputation?

Chapter 18 – Key Insights & Reflections

"If your presence doesn't make an impact then your absence won't make a difference."
- Anonymous

SERVICE, STRENGTH, SUCCESS

James Edwards, also known as the "Most Valuable Motivator," had an extremely challenging path to success. At one point in his life, he would've been considered a complete failure by most standards. A lifetime of struggle and reckless behavior reached a point of crisis in 2005, when James was arrested and charged with the intent to possess and intent to deliver 50-150 kilos of cocaine and 2,000 pounds of marijuana. He pled guilty and was sentenced to 96 months in federal prison. Even though he was in prison serving time, James chose to direct his mind and his focus to working toward his goals. James devoted himself to self-discovery and living for his higher purpose, and when he was released from prison he dedicated his life to serving, inspiring, and empowering others. Now, he travels the world, sharing the story of how God changed his life and spreading his motivational message.

Failure is not the opposite of success. The opposite of success is quitting. Leaders can fail multiple times and still become successful, but when they quit, they lose every time. It takes strength to stay the course when you feel like quitting. I'm talking about inner strength and strength of heart, which is built through believing in yourself and the service that you're here to offer. When you quit, you're giving up on yourself. Quitting is the same as saying "I don't believe in myself, my gifts, or my service." When you believe in yourself, you have the strength to carry on, no matter what may be happening around you. The reason James Edwards could reinvent himself was he believed in his gift and didn't quit.

> Effective leaders build systems for success and pass them on to their successors as examples to follow.

Effective leaders know how to build systems for

success. They take a long, hard looks at their failures and determine what went wrong and then develop a smarter and stronger course of action. Leaders don't settle for mediocrity or partial success. They sacrifice and work hard in order to achieve true success.

The S's of Leadership

Leaders analyze their shortcomings and use their findings to create systems for success.

Leaders can find the sunshine on cloudy days by seeing the positive in negative situations.

Leaders are willing to sacrifice and serve.

Smart leaders realize serving the people they lead is their strongest position because it builds loyalty and gives them a strong rapport with the people they're leading.

Leaders are able to identify their strengths and the strengths of others.

Leaders learn how to turn strains and stresses into success.

Leaders can turn struggles into strengths by properly assessing past failures and mistakes.

Effective leaders build systems for success and pass them on to their successors as examples to follow.

Leaders have a choice: they can complain about what they see, or they can create what they want to see.

Leaders know that mediocre people settle for less because they fail to sacrifice and work hard to go after what they really want.

Effective leaders know how to reflect, review, and resolve conflict.

Leaders know they can lead more effectively by relating with others than by controlling others.

Three things that I wish I would have known about leadership before I became a leader:

1. Never give up when you're losing; you may be one step away from success.

2. Your desire to serve is what will give you the strength to succeed.

3. Don't ever let stress and strain keep you from seeing the sunshine.

Guiding Questions

Have you ever given up on yourself and your success?

What is your greatest strength, and how do you use that strength to be of service to others?

Chapter 19 – Key Insights & Reflections

"The thinking that has brought me this far has produced a problem that this thinking cannot solve."
- Albert Einstein

TEACHABLE, TRUTHFUL, TEAM-ORIENTED

We've all encountered highly talented individuals who just can't seem to create success for themselves. Even though they have all the right gifts, talents, and abilities, they just can't seem to get anywhere. It's certainly not because they don't have what it takes to become successful, or they don't have the potential to become great. I've seen athletes who should be in the NBA playing on neighborhood playgrounds, and I've seen great musicians and producers who should be getting Grammy's playing at local clubs for 25 people every week.

We've all witnessed those individuals who are less talented, but continue to improve with time and dedication and seem to get opportunity after opportunity. Leaders can identify when talented people are teachable and help them get to the next level. Great leaders seek to create a culture and a climate that fosters teaching and learning. Some leaders take time out daily, weekly, or monthly to get input from the people they lead. When employees, volunteers, or team members feel like they are being heard, they are much more open to being taught and coached.

> Leaders watch their tone, temperament, and timing whenever they talk. How we say what we say, when we say what we say, and the tone that we use are all important.

Leaders have to accept the fact that some people are not coachable. Some employees are not team players. We have all seen it in sports. The kid with the greatest natural ability has the worst attitude, or in business, the sales representative with the highest sales and strongest talent is the most self-serving and the least coachable. Even though these types may win the individual awards and accolades, no one wants to play on the team with them. This is why leaders need to be team-oriented. Great leaders are skilled at developing team chemistry that allows all the players to feel valued.

By being truthful in their dealings with others, leaders create a team dynamic of responsibility, accountability, and fairness. Leaders are truthful about their personal strengths and shortcomings, they're truthful with themselves about the strengths and shortcomings of their team, and they're truthful with those around them. Truth-telling and transparency are key habits for leaders, because they create an environment of trust that supports people in giving their best, being their best, and stepping up to play their role.

Effective leaders use their T.I.M.E. wisely. Most people use their T.I.M.E. for TV, Internet, Movies, and Entertainment. Leaders are best served when they use their T.I.M.E. being Trained, Instructed, Motivated, and Educated. One of the defining characteristics of those who lead effectively is how they spend their time.

> **Team-oriented leaders understand the difference between a thermostat and a thermometer – one sets the temperature while the other one only tells the temperature.**

How do you spend your TIME?

TV		Training
Internet	OR	Instruction
Movies		Motivation
Entertainment		Education

The T's of Leadership

Leaders are truthful in their thoughts, words, and deeds, and choose to be fair and honest in their dealings with people.

Leaders have a teachable spirit – they love to teach others and be taught, to lead others and be led.

Leaders tackle difficult issues with tact and tenacity.

Leaders do what needs to be done today without procrastinating.

Leaders must be team-oriented with motives focused on service, not task-oriented with motives focused on self. Leaders know that they don't need a title to be a true leader.

Leaders watch their tone, temperament, and timing whenever they talk. How we say what we say, when we say what we say, and the tone that we use when we say it are all important.

Leaders who have talent and great leadership traits but fail to work hard can only be mediocre.

Leaders who have talent, great leadership traits and work hard are unstoppable.

Effective leaders transform their tomorrow through what they believe and do today.

Team-oriented leaders understand the difference between a thermostat and a thermometer – one sets the temperature while the other one only shows the temperature.

Three things that I wish I would have known about leadership before I became a leader:

1. Teach the value of every position on the team – every team member has a role and responsibility.

2. Be truthful with yourself about the character and capacity of your team members.

3. The team vision is always stronger than the individual vision.

Guiding Questions

What do you do when you recognize someone has great talent but is not teachable?

How can you more effectively use your T.I.M.E. to Train, Instruct, Motivate, and Educate yourself as a leader?

Chapter 20 – Key Insights & Reflections

CHAPTER 21

"It's hard to uplift the team spirit when the Leader is down and out."
- Mansfield Key III

UNDERSTANDING, UNIQUE, UPLIFTING

A leader's unique positive spirit and beliefs can be contagious, especially during times when the team needs to be uplifted. Sometimes, the leader must assure everyone by offering a clear picture and projection of the future. If leaders are unaware of what it costs their team to produce and perform, it makes the team unstable and uncertain. Leaders must understand what they are asking for, and be prepared to handle the process that leads to the results and rewards that they're seeking.

It's very important that leaders be aware and understanding of what is going on in the lives of the people they lead. When Martin Luther King, Jr. made his famous "I Have a Dream" speech, he knew the heart and the desperation of the people he was speaking to at that time. Martin Luther King was able to use his unique strengths and spirit as a leader to uplift the people who followed him, even in the darkest of times. Leaders understand that their own uniqueness is a beacon and an inspiration for the people they lead. Some leaders allow their fear of embarrassment to keep their desire to succeed from evolving.

> Leaders who know more than they understand are not as effective as leaders who understand what they know and can apply it.

The U's of Leadership

Leaders uplift and motivate others through their words and deeds.

Leaders know how to be understanding of their people, process, and projects.

To be a dominant leader in their field, leaders must show up in their unique style and position.

Leaders unite to show unconditional love.

Everyday leaders must be unanimous in mind, body, and spirit, showing love and appreciation, not favoritism.

Leaders are upfront with themselves and others.

Leader's beliefs can uplift the spirit of the team.

Leaders who know more than they understand are not as effective as leaders who understand what they know and can apply it.

Ineffective leaders are unaware, unprepared, and unavailable to the people they lead, and that breeds uncertainty.

Leaders are never unfair in what they practice and are definitely not unfair with the people they lead.

Leaders identify their uniqueness and express that uniqueness as leadership strengths. They then establish a dominant advantage in that area.

Three things that I wish I would have known about leadership before I became a leader:

1. Gaining knowledge is one thing, but understanding how to apply it is golden.

2. Cultivate your own uniqueness. It is one of your keys to leadership.

3. Stay positive. Uplift yourself and uplift others.

Guiding Questions

In what areas of your life, both personal and professional, can you work toward being more positive and uplifting?

Do you understand the unique needs and circumstances of the people you're leading?

Chapter 21 – Key Insights & Reflections

CHAPTER 22

"A clear vision of the future will help you get a clear path to the vision in the present."
- Mansfield Key III

VISUALIZE, VERBALIZE, VALIDATE

The 2013 NBA championship series was between the Miami Heat and the San Antonio Spurs. It was a seven game series, and Miami was down three games to two. In the final seconds of game six, Miami was down by five points. The game and the series appeared to be over. People had begun to leave the arena. But then, something magical happened. San Antonio missed a free throw that would have sealed the deal, Miami got the ball and, with just a few seconds left on the clock, hit a three pointer that sent the game into overtime. Miami went on to win that game and the final series. When Lebron James was asked what was Miami's key to victory, he answered, "We kept visualizing victory, even in the face of defeat."

Leaders visualize the victory, and they are committed to verbalizing their vision from a place of victory instead of a victim mentality. A victim blames others for what "happened to them"; a victorious leader knows that everything is a choice, and recognizes and is responsible for their reality in every choice. The strongest voice in a leader's ears is the voice of their own conscience. This voice is the one that will verbally validate and affirm them in the same way that they must verbally validate others. Leaders truly value and see the worth of the people who they lead, and they speak to what they see. Unless they can see and validate the value of a person or project, then they can't contribute or add any new value or growth.

> **Leaders understand that their voices speak the vision that adds the value that inspires those listening to become victorious.**

7 Keys to Victory

Leaders have a Vision of where they are going.

Leaders are able to Verbalize how they're going to get there.

Leaders see the Victory before the fight.

Leaders should always add Value to the people who they are leading.

Leaders Validate the people they lead.

Leaders are led by the right inner Voice.

Leaders know when and when not to be Vulnerable.

The V's of Leadership

Leaders understand that anything valuable has a cost.

Leaders are able to verbally express the values that lead to productivity.

Leaders validate and affirm others for their work.

Leaders must be able to identify vain pursuits and cease them immediately in order to seek out valuable pursuits.

Leaders with no vision are like pilots with no map or sense of direction steering a plane aimlessly through the air.

Leaders can clearly verbalize the steps of the journey to the people they're leading.

Leaders who have less influence and strong vision are still more effective than leaders with strong influence and no vision.

Leaders must use their voices to speak their vision to the people around them.

Leaders know they can never succeed or add value from a victim mentality.

Leaders can connect the vision to a victorious plan of action.

Leaders understand their voices speak the vision that adds the value that inspires those listening to become victorious.

Leaders understand the most visible and the most verbal person in their life is not always the most valuable person in their life.

Leaders must be able to stimulate people both visually and verbally.

Three things that I wish I would have known about leadership before I became a leader:

1. Always visualize victory, especially in the face of defeat.

2. Use validation to bring value to yourself and the people you lead.

3. Know when to let yourself be vulnerable and when not to be vunerable.

Guiding Questions

Are there any areas where you are still trapped in a victim mentality?

How can you add more value to yourself and others? In what areas can you validate yourself and others?

Chapter 22 – Key Insights & Reflections

CHAPTER 23

"The most important words a leader will ever speak are not to the people he leads, but to himself, in the small, quiet voice of his own wise conscience."
- Unknown

WISDOM, WILLINGNESS, WORK ETHIC

Everyone is capable of wishing for things to happen. We've been taught to make wishes on our birthday candles every year. Leaders have many dreams and visions that they want to bring to reality. What distinguishes a leader from the rest is that they don't just wish and wait; they wish and get to work.

I had a wish that I would write and publish a book one day. For years, I would come up with ideas and concepts and titles. I would talk with other people about it all the time. "I'm getting ready to write a book," I'd say. "I wish I had the time to just sit down and write the entire book." I did this for so long that, finally, my wife said to me, "If you would use all the time that you spend wishing and waiting on actually working, then you'd have the book finished by now!" In that moment, I realized that without work ethic and willingness to follow through, my wishing was worthless.

Willingness means having the desire to do something and being prepared to take action on it. If you are willing to lead, that means that you have the desire to lead and are prepared to step up to the task. It's been said that a leader is simply someone who is willing to stand up and stand out. Leaders are also willing to correct and address the behaviors that are counter-productive to their success, and to admit their mistakes and shortcomings. Willingness is all about being prepared to do whatever it takes, which, in the end, always comes back to doing the inner work and growth.

Having a strong work ethic means understanding the moral benefit and importance of work and its inherent ability to strengthen character. In the lives of leaders, work ethic is the code of conduct that they follow so that others can follow the code with them. Leaders will reproduce themselves in the people they lead.

Effective leaders work with a wisdom that provides the right direction, instruction, and timing.

Direction - *knowing what to do.*
Instruction - *knowing how to do it.*
Timing - *knowing exactly when to do it.*

If every leader embraced these three concepts in every decision, then they would make better choices.

> Leaders express what they want, why they want it, and what they are willing to do to get it.

True wisdom is knowing how to make the right decision for the right reasons. We've seen many smart, influential leaders make poor decisions. Most of these leaders possessed knowledge and lacked wisdom. It's been said that knowledge can be gained through information and education, but wisdom only comes through experience. With knowledge, you have useful facts and information, but with wisdom you have the ability to consistently apply that knowledge toward making good life decisions.

Leaders should be grateful for the strength and guidance they've been given, and for the help they receive in their times of weakness. To lead with knowledge and without higher wisdom is dangerous. The strongest and most connected leaders are connected with a higher wisdom that they apply to their lives, both personally and professionally.

The W's of Leadership

Leaders expose themselves to the knowledge of others but choose to follow their own wisdom.

With the wisdom that comes through experience, leaders can lead through good instincts and intuition.

Leaders are willing to identify their strengths and work on their weaknesses.

Leaders know the difference between waiting for something and working toward something.

Leaders express what they want, why they want it, and what they are willing to do to get it.

A leader's work ethic produces consistent results.

Leaders who are not willing to stand up and stand out forfeit their right to lead.

A leader's work should validate and affirm who they are.

Leaders apply wisdom and willingly demonstrate a strong work ethic through the way that they live and lead.

Leaders change their world and the world of the people they lead with their words.

Leaders don't worry because they understand worrying is a misuse of their mind and their time.

Three things that I wish I would have known about leadership before I became a leader:

1. You need both knowledge and experience to apply true wisdom.

2. Wishing and waiting without working leads to great conversation and zero results.

3. Being able and being willing to lead are two different things.

Guiding Questions

Do you have the willingness and work ethic to make your wishes become reality?

How can you lead with both knowledge and wisdom?

Chapter 23 – Key Insights & Reflections

CHAPTER 24

"The best executive is the one who has sense enough to pick good men to do what he wants done, and self-restraint enough to keep from meddling with them while they do it." - Theodore Roosevelt

X-RAY

All leaders must x-ray their lives to scan for people, places, and things that get in the way of their growth. Just like an anti-virus program that scans for infected files and deletes them so that a computer can run at optimum speed, leaders must examine their personal and professional lives for negative influences. Leaders x-ray people, projects, and the overall process for positivity and progress.

When leaders x-ray people and projects, it simply

means that they're taking a closer look at what's going on beneath the surface. While an x-ray of a person's body might reveal broken bone, torn tissue, or an unnatural growth that needs to be immediately addressed to improve the patient's condition, a leader's x-ray reveals where the project, people, or team needs to improve. Ineffective leaders rarely x-ray the project and the team's progression, going on the assumption that everything is going according to plan. Appearances can be misleading, however, an effective leader must be able to examine what's going on below the surface.

Leaders can x-ray a situation to determine if a person is helping and supporting the team, or if they're bringing negative habits and destructive influence into the project. There are thoughts, actions, and behaviors that lead to distraction and destruction, and leaders know how to identify those in others because they are skilled at examining themselves. At one point on my path to leadership, I did a thorough x-ray on myself to scan my own methods, motives, and mission. I was shocked by what I found. This intense self-investigation revealed to me that I had been doing the right things for the wrong reasons. Now, I have become more aware when other people have hidden agendas and mixed motives.

Everyone has both positive and negative influences

somewhere in their lives. For some people, it's family, and for others it may be co-workers, friends, or colleagues. Most people have negative thoughts that influence their behaviors and beliefs, and some people work consciously to cultivate positive thoughts, behaviors, and relationships that will direct them toward their destiny. Leaders are aware and able to track whether negativity or positivity is influencing their actions and direction.

> Leaders must x-ray their lives to scan for people, beliefs, and behaviors that inhibit their growth.

Motivational speaker Jim Rohn said we are each the average of the five people who we spend the most time. We all need both positive reinforcement and constructive criticism to grow. If you x-ray the five people closest to you, can you see whether they are helping or hindering your progress?

The X's of Leadership

Leaders must x-ray their lives to scan for people, beliefs, and behaviors that inhibit their growth.

Leaders know how to examine both their personal and

professional lives for positive and negative influences.

When leaders identify what needs to be done, they must have the courage to do it.

Leaders know how to look beyond the surface of the people and the project to get a closer view of what's going on inside.

Based on what they see during examinations of their people and projects, leaders are able to make an honest assessment and decide what's needed for progress.

Leaders are able to determine whether a person is leading the team and the project toward destiny or destruction.

True leaders self-examine their own weaknesses and use that information to build a strong team.

When leaders x-ray the habits of themselves and the people they lead, it often reveals hidden motives for wanting to fulfill the mission.

Leaders should regularly take the time to x-ray and examine themselves and look honestly at what they see.

Leaders are able to determine whether the people closest to them are supporting or slowing down their progress.

Three things that I wish I would have known about leadership before I became a leader:

1. X-ray your life for people, projects, and habits that support your destiny.

2. X-ray your life for people, projects, and habits that lead to distraction and detours.

3. X-ray all of your projects to identify both positive and negative influences.

Guiding Questions

Are you effectively x-raying your relationships, projects, and personal habits to identify the ones that truly support your greater purpose?

If you x-ray the five people closest to you, what do you see about how their habits and beliefs affect your leadership style?

Chapter 24 – Key Insights & Reflections

The yoke you wear determines the burden you bear.
- Edwin Louis Cole

YEARN, YES, YIELD

One of the aspects of leadership that draws leaders to lead is their yearning to create a better world in some way, big or small. Leaders must listen to their hearts and say yes to this yearning. When leaders fail to follow their yearning to make the world a better place for the right reasons, they get yoked to the wrong people and projects.

A yoke is a wooden crosspiece that is fastened over the necks of two animals and attached to a plow or cart that the animals pull. Yoked animals are at the mercy of whoever is operating the plow. If leaders are stubborn and unyielding or don't listen to what their hearts and minds are saying yes to, they can get yoked to yesterday's influences in the form of destructive thoughts, people, and projects. Yesterday's yoke can prevent leaders from acting and operating in the area of their present strengths and gifts.

It could be a past failure, a past success, or past missed opportunity that keeps you yoked to yesterday. There have been many times that I yoked myself to yesterday's events as if they still had control over my future. The truth is every moment is new, the past event is over, and we must find a way to move on. The divorce is final. The project failed. You were fired. The company didn't succeed. You filed for bankruptcy. The song was a flop. Whatever it was or whatever it is, it's all a valuable experience for greater growth and opportunity. The past is gone, regardless of how bad or how good it was, and the future is always brighter if you look for it. Instead of keeping yourself yoked to yesterday, follow your heart's yearning for a brighter tomorrow.

> Leaders don't just yearn to make a difference; they learn to be the difference.

Great leaders understand following their heart's

yearning doesn't mean enforcing their personal will on others. In saying yes to their dreams, leaders also know how and when to yield and say yes to others. It takes a strong spirit to yield a personal agenda over to the greatest good of the whole, and leaders must be able to do just that. When you say yes to a greater vision, you learn to yield your personal desires for the higher good of the team and the mission.

The Y's of Leadership

Leaders listen to and act on their yearning for the right thing instead of getting yoked to the wrong thing.

Leaders don't just yearn to make a difference; they learn to be the difference.

Leaders understand they must be willing to let go of yesterday's methods and strategies in order to find tomorrow's mission and solutions.

Leaders listen to their hearts and say yes to their yearning.

When leaders are stubborn and unyielding or don't listen

to what their hearts are saying yes to, they can get yoked to yesterday's influences.

Leaders are willing to stand up and say yes to the test, the task, and the training of the call to lead.

Leaders know when and how to yield their personal will to the needs of the team, the project, and the vision.

Some leaders yearn for the perks and prestige that come with leadership, but don't want to say yes to the pain, the problems, and the process of it.

Leaders that say yes to being a leader, but say no to the growth development process, is a sure recipe for disaster.

Leaders are able to yield their power and control over to others when it's appropriate.

Leaders must be willing to yield convenience and comfort and say yes to embracing change for progress.

Three things that I wish I would have known about leadership before I became a leader:

1. Say yes to the present by letting go of what yoked you to the past.

2. You are the leader you've been waiting for – say yes to you.

3. Support today's yearning by taking steps to prepare for the future.

Guiding Questions

What is your heart yearning for, and are you saying yes to it?

What personal desires can you yield for the sake of your greater vision?

Chapter 25 – Key Insights & Reflections

"Zeal without knowledge is fire without light."
- Thomas Fuller

ZESTY, ZEALOUS, ZANY

People are drawn to leaders because of their zest and zeal, which is the strong emotional energy and dedication that drives them to bring their visions to life. Sometimes when leaders are pursuing a big dream, they can get sidetracked going after every promising opportunity or connection and lose sight of the forest for the trees. This kind of behavior turns even the strongest leader into a zany caricature. Zany leaders are like clowns or comedians, mimicking others, moving like a puppet in the position of leadership instead of true leader. They will follow every management fad or trend without truly understanding the people who they are leading or the goals that they are trying to accomplish.

Leaders who possess true zeal can sustain passion for their purpose and projects beyond that first burst of energy and excitement. Zeal shows up as great energy and enthusiasm in pursuit of a greater cause, and it's a quality that's important for leaders to possess when they have a team to inspire. When you are motivated and compelled by a vision, you're zealous not for yourself, but for your entire team, and for everyone who that vision will impact. A zealous leader who builds a team can easily attract and inspire others to the vision and mission of the project.

> Leaders are motivated and zealous for the success of the team, not just themselves.

To be zany is to play the clown or the fool for the sake of amusing others. When pleasing and amusing others becomes more important than leading people, that means leadership has become a popularity contest. You see this sometimes with politicians who are inauthentic, playing the role that they think people want them to play in order to get votes. As a leader, it's great to support your team with a sense of humor – it uplifts people and keeps them feeling connected. However, becoming a comical caricature in an effort to be liked is not healthy, nor is it what being a leader is about.

The Z's of Leadership

Leaders are zealous in their vision and purpose, but not zany.

When zealous leaders are operating in their gifts, they will inspire others.

A leader's zeal shows up as energy, enthusiasm, and passion for their purpose.

Zesty leaders possess a lively, pleasant approach to life.

Leaders are motivated and zealous for the success of the team, not just themselves.

Balanced leaders know when to be zesty, innovative, and creative, and when to keep the status quo.

Zany leaders have sacrificed the attributes of a true leader in favor of being liked by the crowd.

If leaders express their zeal without wisdom or knowledge, they will wind up leading the right people in the wrong way.

Three things that I wish I would have known about leadership before I became a leader:

1. The zeal of a true leader is not motivated by individual success, but by team success.

2. Zest and zeal will take you far, but must be balanced with experience and wisdom.

3. Acting zany in order to be liked will never get you to where you actually want to go.

Guiding Questions

Have you ever compromised your values in order to be liked?

In what areas of your personal and professional life are you most passionately full of zest and zeal?

Chapter 26 – Key Insights & Reflections

Make your anger so expensive
that no one can afford it,
and make your happiness so
cheap that people can
almost get it for free.

- Anonymous

EPILOGUE

Now that you have completed ***Key's ABC's to Leadership*** it is time to lead. Regardless of your title, whether it is with a school, church, business or just you and your family, it's time to lead. Review the letters that stood out the most for you and apply them to your life. Our goal was to educate, equip, and empower you with tools you can apply to the style of leadership that works for you.

As a leader, it's important that we identify our style and see what is most effective for the people, projects, and programs we are leading. One style may be great for leading people but not with leading a particular project or implementing a new program. ***Key's ABC's*** are designed to help you motivate your team to be effective and efficient. Leaders must be able to envision the future and convince others that their vision is worth following.

Communication is key and getting the people you lead to focus on one common goal by creating and cultivating the right environment. When the leader creates the atmosphere that brings out the best and inspires people to give their best for the sake of the team, it will also motivate them to perform at high levels.

Most leaders have some natural leadership abilities and characteristics, but *Key's ABC's* will help them guide, guard, and govern the people they lead and themselves. When people are linked, locked, and latched on to the person and the purpose or vision, they will go where you lead. When they are not connected to the person, purpose or vision, they will not follow.

Ultimately as a Leader you must make other people better and help them get to a place they would not have gone to without you. Whether it's a Fortune 500 company, a school, a church, or your family, the goal is to dream more, learn more, do more, and become more. If your actions as a leader does that, then you are officially a leader. Lead!

Now it is time for you to do like that 7th grade student you read about in the prologue who did not want to go home and face his dad. He stood up and did what the others did not have the courage to do. He did what the others were thinking but were afraid to do. He did what most people do every day when they look for someone else to do it. He stepped up, stepped forward and led everyone else to do the right thing. I am asking you to do the same. Step up and do the right thing, and just like the other players on my team that eventually followed my example, there are others waiting to come forth when they see you.

I leave you with two questions to ponder:

What kind of mark will your leadership make while you're living?

What kind of legacy will your leadership leave when you die?

Only you can answer those questions, but this book has hopefully helped you develop the skills to do it more efficiently and effectively. The ultimate goal as a leader is to HOPE (Help Other People Excel).

BIO

Mansfield Key III, known to most as Ole Pete Key, is a Author, a coach, consultant, speech writer, certified HIV/AIDS Instructor, social entrepreneur, and mentor. Mr. Key is an International Motivational Speaker who is a leading Growth Development Strategist. He has impacted the lives of over a million people through presentations, programs, and products. His proudest accomplishment other than his relationship with God is his devotion to his loving wife, Sharlene. He is the proud father of two beautiful daughters Erin Ruth and Joi Da'Nae.

He has provided technical assistance to the Federal Government's Health and Human Service for all 50 states. He has worked directly with The CDC (Centers for Disease Control) in the United States. Pete has also completed consultant work for the Department of Education, Department of Public Health, The Juvenile Justice System, The Foster Care System, the Dream Development Center in Johannesburgh South Africa and Livepool England's Hope Organization. He has also provided Cultural Awareness Training for Police & Fire Departments. He has spoken at the Ryan White National Conference, the Steve Harvey

Mentoring Camp for boys, SAMSA (Substance Abuse and Mental Health Services Administration), NASTAD (National Alliance of State Territorial AIDS Directors) and many more.

While Pete has been successful in many endeavors, he is mostly known for his ability to use music, drama, and motivational teachings to educate and empower people to unlock their potential and determine their destiny. His character Ray Ray, the Drop-Out Bully has been presented at thousands of presentations and impacted lives in schools, churches, and community centers.

Pete has accomplished several things professionally but his personal life was a complete disaster. The kid who grew up on the wrong side of the tracks in a small city called Florence Alabama has not always been a positive person. He spent years of promiscuous living experimenting with alcohol, drugs, and sex after he dropped out of college. In school he couldn't read, so he struggled tremendously until a teacher name Ms. Stockard gave him some life changing advice. She introduced him to someone who would help him. She also gave him a method to help him overcome his weaknesses in school. He is still benefiting from Ms. Stockard's advice. It is priceless to him.

His purpose and passion today is sharing his story and strategies to help others. He believes that everyone has something special, but sometime people just need others to help them discover it. He said he wanted to be a "Ms. Stockard" to someone else in need because he believes that "Someone's Destiny is connected to our Assignment."

KEY'S ABC'S OF LEADERSHIP

GLOSSARY

A

ABANDON: forsaken or deserted
ABILITY: power or capacity to do or act physically, mentally, legally, morally, financially
ABORT: to fail, cease, or stop at an early or premature stage.
ACCOLADES: any award, honor, or laudatory notice
ACCOMPLISHMENTS: anything accomplished; deed; achievement, completed; done; effected
ACCOUNTABLE: the state of being accountable, liable, or answerable
ACHIEVEMENTS: superior ability, special effort, great courage, etc.; a great or heroic deed
ACKNOWLEDGE: to admit to be real or true; recognize the existence, truth, or fact of
ACTION: something done or performed; act; deed
ACTIVITY: a specific deed, action, function, or sphere of action
ADAPT: to make suitable to requirements or conditions; adjust or modify fittingly
ADJUST: to change (something) so that it fits, or conforms; adapt; accommodate
ADVERSITY: a condition marked by misfortune, calamity, or distress
AFFIRMATION: a statement or proposition that is declared to be true
ALERT: fully aware and attentive; wide-awake; keen
ALTER: to make different in some particular, as size, style, course, or the like; modify
ATTITUDE: manner, disposition, feeling, position, with regard to a person or thing
AUDIBLE: a play called at the line of scrimmage to supersede the play originally agreed upon as the result of a change in strategy.
AVAILABLE: fully aware and attentive; wide-awake; keen
AWARE: informed, having knowledge; conscious; cognizant

B

BUILD: to construct, by assembling and joining parts and materials, to mold, form, create
BRAND: kind, grade, or make, stamped, trademarked, or the like
BUSY: actively and attentively engaged in work or a pastime
BALANCE: a state of equilibrium or equipoise; equal distribution of weight, amount, etc.

BEING: the fact of existing; existence, conscious
BLESSED: divinely or supremely favored, fortunate, worthy
BEST: of the highest quality, excellence, or standing
BELIEVE: to have confidence in the truth, the existence, or the reliability of something, although without absolute proof that one is right in doing so
BETTER: of superior quality or excellence, greater
BLAME: to place the responsibility for (a fault, error, etc.)
BOAST: to speak with exaggeration and excessive pride, especially about oneself
BUCK: to pass (something) along to another, as a means of avoiding responsibility or blame

C
CALLING: vocation, profession, or trade, or a strong impulse, or inclination
CAPABLE: having power and ability; efficient; competent
CAREER: an occupation or profession, especially one requiring special training, followed as one's lifework
CAUSE: a person or thing that acts, happens, or exists in such a way that some specific thing happens as a result; the producer of an effect
CHANGE: to make different from what it is or from what it would be if left alone, transform, convert
CLIMATE: the prevailing attitudes, standards, or environmental conditions of a group, period, or place
COACHABLE: a person who is able to be trained, instructed, and molded
COINCIDENCE: a striking occurrence of two or more events at one time apparently by mere chance
COLLABORATE: to work, one with another; cooperate, as on a literary work
COMPETENT: having suitable or sufficient skill, knowledge, experience, properly qualified
COMMITTED: to pledge (oneself) to a position on an issue or question; express
COMMUNICATE: to impart knowledge of; make known, transmit
CONFIDENCE: full trust; belief in the powers, or reliability of a person or thing
CONFLICT: collision, controversy, quarrel, clash, disagreement, in opposition
CONFRONT: to face in hostility or defiance; oppose
CONNECTION: anything that connects;that connects connecting that part; link; bond
CONSISTENTLY: agreeing or accordant; compatible; not self-contradictory
CONVICTIONS: a fixed or firm belief
COOPERATE: to work or act together or jointly for a common purpose or benefit.
COST: the price paid to acquire, produce, accomplish, or maintain anything

COURAGE: the quality of mind or spirit that enables a person to face difficulty, danger, pain, etc., without fear; bravery
COURAGEOUSLY: possessing or characterized by courage; brave
CREATE: to cause to come into being, as something unique that would not naturally evolve or that is not made by ordinary processes
CULTURE: the behaviors and beliefs, characteristic of a particular social, ethnic, or age group

D
DEDICATED: wholly committed to something, an ideal, political cause, or personal goal
DEFINE: the meaning that explains, or identify the nature or essential qualities
DELAYED: to put off to a later time; defer; postpone
DETERMINED: decided, settled, resolved
DELAYED: to put off to a later time; defer; postpone:
DESIGN: to form or conceive in the mind; contrive; plan
DESTINY: something that is to happen or has happened to a particular person or thing; lot or fortune, predetermined, usually inevitable
DESIGN: to form or conceive in the mind; contrive; plan
DETOUR: roundabout, or circuitous way or course, indirect route
DIRECTION: instruction or guidance for making, using, etc.; management, control
DISCIPLINED: having or exhibiting discipline; rigorous
DISTRACTED: having the attention diverted

E
EDUCATED: to qualify by instruction or training for a particular calling, practice, etc.; train
ELIMINATE: do away with, banish, abolish, eradicate, erase, exterminate, cut out, stamp out
EMPOWERED: to enable or permit
ENCOURAGED: to stimulate (something or someone) by approval or help; support
ENCOURAGEMENT: praise, support, boost, lift, endorsement
ENLIGHTEN: to give information or understanding to; instruct; edify
ETHIC: The rules or standards governing the conduct of a person
EXAMPLE: a pattern or model, as of something to be imitated or avoided
EXCUSES: to release from an obligation or duty
EXPOSED: to make known, disclose, or reveal (intentions, secrets, etc.)

F

FAILURES: a person or thing that is unsuccessful or disappointing
FAMILY: a basic social unit consisting of parents and their children, considered as a group
FAITHFUL: true to one's word, promises, vows, etc
FINANCE: the monetary resources, or individual; revenue
FINISH: the end or conclusion; the final part or last stage
FITNESS: Condition of being physically healthy, from exercise and proper nutrition
FLAWS: an imperfection, defect, or blemish
FOCUS: to concentrate
FOLLOW: to conform to, comply with, or act in accordance with; obey
FORGIVE: to cease to feel resentment against
FRUITFUL: producing an abundant growth, as of fruit
FRUITION: the attainment or realization of something worked for or desired; fulfillment

G

GIFTS: a special ability or capacity; natural endowment; talent
GLOW: The sensation or perception of such energy as warmth or hotness
GO: to move or proceed, to or from a point or in a certain direction
GOOD: satisfactory in quality, quantity, or degree
GREAT: unusual or considerable in degree, power, intensity, etc
GROW: to bring to full development
GUTS: Courage; nerve

H

HABITS: an acquired behavior, pattern, regularly followed
HARDENED: to become rigid or unyielding; stiffen
HEAL: to make healthy, whole, or sound; restore to health; free from ailment
HELPING: giving aid, assistance, support, or the like
HOPING: to look forward to with desire and reasonable confidence.
HUMBLE: not proud or arrogant; modest
HUMILITY: modest opinion or estimate of one's own importance, rank, etc
HURTING: to cause mental pain to; offend or grieve

I

IMAGINE: to think, believe, or guess
IMMEDIATELY: without lapse of time; without delay; instantly; at once

KEY'S ABC'S OF LEADERSHIP

IMPACT: influence; effect
IMPOSSIBLE: unable to be done, performed, effected, etc.
IDENTIFY: to associate with another person or a group of persons by identification
INDIVIDUALLY: one at a time; separately
INFLUENCE: an effect of one person or thing on another
IGNITING: to stimulate or provoke
INSPIRE: the action or process of producing effects on the actions, behavior, opinions, etc.
INTERNALLY: coming or acting from within; interior
INVEST: to use, give, or devote (time, talent, etc.), as for a purpose or to achieve something
INVESTIGATE: to make inquiry, examination,
INVOLVED: choosing to involve oneself in or commit oneself to something

J

JESUS: A prophet of the first century of our era; to Christians, Jesus Christ, the son of God, a person who was both God and man, the Messiah sent by God to save the human race from the sin it inherited through the Fall of Man
JOIN: to bring together in a particular relation or for a specific purpose, action, etc.; unite
JOURNEY: passage or progress from one stage to another
JOURNAL: a daily record, as of occurrences, experiences, or observations
JOY: a deep feeling or condition of happiness or contentment
JUGGLE: to keep (several activities) in progress, esp. with difficulty
JUSTIFY: to show a satisfactory reason or excuse for something done

K

KEEN: having or showing great mental penetration or acumen
KEYS: Essential; crucial, affords a means of access, that secures and control
KINDNESS: friendly feeling; liking
KNOW-HOW: knowledge of how to do something; faculty or skill expertise.
KNOWLEDGE: awareness, as of a fact or circumstance

L

LAUGHABLE: to cause laughter; funny; amusing; ludicrous
LEADERS: a person who rules, guides, or inspires others; head
LEARNING: The act, process, or experience of gaining knowledge or skill
LIKABLE: easy to like; pleasing
LIMIT: A confining or restricting object, agent, or influence

LISTENING: to give attention with the ear; attend closely for the purpose of hearing
LOOKING: to use one's sight or vision in seeking, searching, examining, watching, etc.
LYING: a false statement made with deliberate intent to deceive.

M
MANDATORY: Law. Permitting no option; not to be disregarded or modified
MAXIMIZE: to increase to the greatest possible amount or degree
MEASURE: any standard of comparison, estimation, or judgment
MENTALLY: in or with the mind or intellect; intellectually
MENTOR: a wise or trusted adviser or guide
METHODS: means, technique. method, mode, way imply a manner in which a thing is done
MISSION: a goal or purpose that is accompanied by strong conviction; a calling or vocation
MOBILIZE: to organize for a purpose; movement
MODERN: characteristic of present and recent time; contemporary; not antiquated
MOMENTS: a definite period or stage, as in a course of events; juncture
MONETIZE: to give a legal value to (a coin)
MOTIVES: something that causes a person to act in a certain way, do certain things

N
NAVIGATE: to move or progress through something in a logical sequence
NEGOTIATE: to deal or bargain with another or others
NETWORK: an association of individuals having a common interest
NET WORTH: the total assets of a business minus its total liabilities
NEUTRAL: not aligned with or supporting any side or position in a controversy
NIMBLE: quick and light in movement; moving with ease; agile; active; rapid
NOTABLE: a prominent, distinguished, or important person

O
OBSTACLES: something that obstructs or hinders progress
OPINIONS: a personal view, attitude, or appraisal
OPPONENTS: a person who opposes another in a contest, battle, etc
OPPORTUNITIES: an appropriate or favorable time or occasion
OPPOSITION: the act of opposing, or the state of being opposed by way of

comparison
OPTIMUM: the greatest degree or best result obtained under specific conditions
OPTIONS: the power or right of choosing
OUTLETS: a means for release or expression of emotion, creative energy, etc
OVERCOME: to get the better of in a struggle or conflict; conquer; defeat

P
PAIN: mental or emotional suffering or torment
PASSION: a strong affection or enthusiasm for an object, concept, etc
PEAK PERFORMANCE: a state in which the person performs to the maximum of their ability, characterized by subjective feelings of confidence, effortlessness
PERSUASION: a deep conviction or belief
PICTURE: a mental image
PLANNING: a detailed scheme, method, etc, for attaining an objective
POSITIVE: confident in opinion or assertion; fully assured
POSSIBILITIES: the state or fact of being possible
POTENTIAL: capable of being or becoming
POWER: to bring to its goal or conclusion; carry out; perform; finish
PREDICT: to foretell the future
PREPARE: to put things or oneself in readiness; get ready
PRESSURE: to force (someone) toward a particular end; influence
PRIORITY: the right of precedence over others
PROBLEMS: any question or matter involving doubt, uncertainty, or difficulty
PROCESS: a continuous action, operation, or series of changes taking place
PROCRASTINATION: act of putting off or delaying, something requiring immediate attention
PURPOSE: the reason for which something exists or is done, made, used, etc.
PURSUE: to strive to gain; seek to attain or accomplish (an end, object, purpose, etc.)

Q
QUALITY: high grade; superiority; excellence
QUALM: an uneasy feeling or pang of conscience as to conduct; compunction
QUEST: a search or pursuit made in order to find or obtain something
QUESTIONS: words addressed to a person in order to elicit information or evoke a response
QUIETLY: making no noise or sound, especially no disturbing sound
QUITTING: to stop, cease, or discontinue

QUINTESSENTIAL: most typically representative of a quality, state, etc. perfect

R

REACT: to act in a reverse direction or manner
REAL: genuine; not counterfeit, artificial, or imitation; authentic
REBELLION: resistance to or defiance of any authority, control, or tradition
REBOUND: to bound or spring back from force of impact
RECEIVE: to take (something offered) into one's hand or possession
RECOMMIT: to commit again
RECOVER: to make up for or make good
REFLECT: to think, ponder, or meditate
REGRETS: to feel sorrow or remorse
REGULATION: a rule, principle, or condition that governs procedure or behavior
RELATABLE: to establish a social or sympathetic relationship with a person or thing
RELATIONSHIPS: a connection, association, or involvement
RELEASE: to free from confinement, bondage, obligation, pain, etc.; let go
RELEVANT: having direct bearing on the matter in hand; pertinent
RELIABLE: able to be trusted; predictable or dependable
RESOLVE: to come to a determination; make up one's mind; determine
RESOURCES: a supply or source of aid or support; something resorted to in time of need
RESPOND: to reply or answer in words
REVENUE: something that yields a regular financial return; source of income
REVIEW: to view, look at, or look over again
RULE: a law, rule, or other order prescribed by authority, especially to regulate conduct

S

SACRIFICE: a surrender of something of value as a means of gaining something more
SERVE: to render or be of service to (a person, cause, etc.); help
SETTLE: to arrange or be arranged in a fixed or comfortable position
STRENGTHS: power by reason of influence, authority, resources, numbers, etc.
STRUGGLE: to move about strenuously so as to escape from something confining
SUCCESSFUL: marked by a favorable outcome
SUCCESSORS: a person or thing that follows, esp. a person who succeeds another in an office

SUFFERING: feeling pain or distress, to tolerate or allow
SUNSHINE: a source of cheer or happiness
SYSTEM: an assemblage or combination of parts forming a complex or unitary whole

T
TACKLE: to deal with (a person) on some problem, issue, etc
TACTFULNESS: a keen sense of what to say or do to avoid giving offense
TALENTED: a special natural ability or aptitude
TEACHABLE: capable of being instructed, as a person
TEMPERAMENT: the combination of mental, physical, and emotional traits of a person
TENACITY: stubborn or persistent
THERMOSTAT: A device that automatically controls the temperature room
THERMOMETER: an instrument for measuring temperature
TIME: to measure or record the speed, duration, or rate of

U
UNANIMOUS: in complete or absolute agreement
UNAVAILABLE: not obtainable or accessible
UNAWARE: not aware or conscious; unconscious
UNCERTAINTY: unpredictability; indeterminacy; indefiniteness
UNCONDITIONAL: without conditions or limitations
UNDERSTAND: to perceive the meaning of; grasp the idea of; comprehend
UNFAIR: not fair; not conforming to approved standards, as of justice, honesty, or ethics
UNIQUENESS: existing as the only one or as the sole example; single; solitary in type
UPLIFTING: inspirational; offering or providing hope, encouragement, salvation, etc.
UNPREPARED: not made ready or prepared

V
VALIDATE: to give legal force or official confirmation to; declare legally valid
VALUABLE: having qualities worthy of respect, admiration, or esteem
VALUES: to consider with respect to worth, excellence, usefulness, or importance.
VERBALIZE: to express (an idea, feeling, etc) in words
VERBALLY: expressed in spoken words; oral rather than written
VICTORY: a success or superior position achieved against any opponent, opposition

KEY'S ABC'S OF LEADERSHIP

VISION: the act or power of seeing
VISUALIZE: to form a mental image

W

WAITING: to remain inactive or in a state of repose, as until something expected happens
WEAKNESSES: the state or quality of being weak; lack of strength, or the like; feebleness
WILLING: to decide, bring about, or attempt to effect or bring about by an act of the will
WISDOM: knowledge of what is true or right coupled with just judgment as to action
WORK: exertion or effort directed to produce or accomplish something; labor; toil
WORKING: physical or mental effort directed towards doing or making something
WORLD: a particular class of people, with common interests, aims, etc.:
WORRY: a cause of uneasiness or anxiety; trouble

X

X-RAY: a photo, a picture, an image of an internal structure, such as bones, or body parts

Y

YIELD: to give up or surrender, submit, to a power or authority
YEARN: to have an earnest or strong desire
YOKED: to join, to couple, to link, to unite, like two animals attached by a wooden frame

Z

ZEALOUS: filled with or inspired by intense enthusiasm
ZANY: one who plays the clown or fool in order to amuse others
ZESTY: energetic; active, liveliness or energy; animating spirit

HOW DO I GIVE MY BEST PROFESSIONALLY WHEN I DON'T FEEL MY BEST PERSONALLY?

HOW DO YOU GIVE YOUR STUDENTS, CLIENTS, OR CUSTOMERS...

SUNSHINE
ON A CLOUDY DAY?

We Provide:
* STAFF DEVELOPMENT
* ASSEMBLY PROGRAMS
* KEYNOTE ADDRESSES
* WORKSHOPS FOR YOUTH, ADULTS CHURCHES, CORPORATIONS, SCHOOLS & NON-PROFIT ORGANIZATIONS.

BOOK MANSFIELD KEY TODAY!

THE 5 I'S OF INSPIRATION | THE 3 M'S OF MOTIVATION | THE 4 L'S OF LEADERSHIP

WWW.OLEPETEKEY.COM

Coming Soon...

The 4 P's to Hope

Key's ABC's
for Christian Leadership

The HOPE Project
*Someone's Destiny is Tied
to Your Assignment*

Beyond Your Imagination

Better Together Project

Key's ABC's *to Leadership* Bundle Pack

www.keysabcs.com